AF483261

Trusting God's Lead, When the World Pulls You Away

FOLLOW THE CLOUD, NOT THE CROWD

DARYL REED

Printed in the United States of America.
First Edition: 2026

Hardback ISBN: 979-8-9938782-3-2
Paperback ISBN: 979-8-9938782-2-5

Library of Congress Control Number 2026900585

Cover Design & Interior Typesetting: Jonathan Lewis

Published by Still Waters Media LLC, Silver Spring, MD.
www.DarylReed.com

DEDICATION

To my Lord and Savior, Christ Jesus — my true Groom,
the One who found me in the fog, steadied my steps,
and led me with a cloud by day and mercy through the night.
Each page in this book is an offering back to Your relentless grace.

And to Charon — my Bride,
God's gift for the journey,
the heart beside mine through wilderness winds and promised horizons.
Your love has been the steady strength beneath every step
and the gentle echo of God's kindness in my life.

CONTENTS

INTRODUCTION

When the Cloud Moves

YOU DON'T NEED a map.

You need the One who goes ahead.

We live in a world that rewards control—and punishes uncertainty.

Plan harder. Grind longer. Lock it all down.

But walking with God teaches a harder truth:

real trust is forged when certainty runs out.

This isn't a book of shortcuts or spiritual formulas.

It's a call to leave the crowd and walk in the presence of God.

God has always led His people this way.

Not by lighting the entire road—

but by giving enough light to stay with Him.

In Exodus 13, Scripture says the Lord went ahead of His people in a pillar of cloud to guide them. That cloud wasn't a signpost. It wasn't a metaphor.

It was God Himself—present, active, moving.

By night, the cloud became a pillar of fire so His people could keep going when vision failed and fear pressed in.

When the cloud stopped, they stopped.

When it rose, they moved.

That is how God leads.

And that is how He still leads.

Not with formulas.

Not with forecasts.

But with His presence.

A Path You Can Walk

This book stays close to that path—moments when God moved, when people hesitated, and when trust was hammered out under pressure.

Some chapters will strengthen you.

Others will confront you.

A few may expose where you've been standing still longer than you realized.

All of them are meant to help you stay anchored and move forward in faith.

You'll encounter a God who:

- leads when the path disappears
- speaks when the crowd gets loud
- waits when impatience takes over
- provides in dry places
- calls the unqualified
- sends the reluctant

You'll also walk alongside people forced to choose:

follow the cloud—or stay with the crowd.

Some followed.

Some folded.

Some surrendered.

Some clung to control.

But through it all, God kept moving.

And here's the part we don't like to admit:

He moved whether they followed or not.

He is still moving now.

Why I Wrote This Book

I didn't write this book because I've mastered trust. I'm still learning.

I wrote it because I've spent enough time in the fog to recognize the moment when conviction begins to slip—not loudly, but quietly, one rational decision at a time.

I've been circling this book for more than twenty years—long before I was ready to write it—watching God ask for trust before He ever gave answers. And this finally became the season to put words to what I've been living.

Along the way, I've watched good people drift with the crowd—and pay for it with their faith. I've seen how mob thinking erodes character, how fear disguises itself as wisdom, and how compromise rarely announces itself until it has already settled in.

I've also seen what happens when someone—imperfect, unsure, unfinished—chooses to stay anchored to God's presence anyway.

Not because the path is clear.

But because the Presence is.

The title of this book was born in those seasons—when certainty was scarce, pressure was constant, and obedience mattered more than explanations. *Follow the Cloud, Not the Crowd* became more than a phrase.

It became a way of living.

My prayer is simple:

that you won't just read these pages but recognize your own moments of hesitation in them—and discover that God has been leading you, even when you couldn't see it.

How to Use This Book

There's no rush here.

Strength is built through repeated obedience.

Each chapter ends with simple, honest tools to help you respond:

- **Cloud Marker** — one truth worth carrying
- **Prayer Prompt** — a moment of submission and resolve
- **Reflection Questions** — space to think deeply and honestly
- **Live It Out** — a concrete act of obedience

Read alone or with others.

Move quickly or take your time.

But don't confuse patience with avoidance.

This book exists to help you follow Someone—not merely learn something.

THIS IS FOR YOU

THIS BOOK IS for those in the fog—
still standing, but tired of guessing.
For those who feel the weight of responsibility—
leaders, parents, servants, builders—
who want to trust God without surrendering strength.
It's for the disciplined and the doubting.
For the weary who refuse to quit.
For those who know control is an illusion but still struggle to release it.
Wherever you are, God is not finished with you.
His presence is still ahead of you.
The next step doesn't require full visibility.
It requires decision.
So don't just read.
Lift your eyes.
Notice where the cloud is moving.
Because when God moves, neutrality is not an option.
And the most dangerous place to stand
is close enough to see the cloud—
but unwilling to follow it.

PART ONE

WHEN GOD GOES FIRST

BEFORE GOD ASKS us to follow, He reveals Himself.

Before He calls for surrender, He offers His presence.

From the beginning, faith has never been about charting a course—it has been about recognizing who goes ahead. In the wilderness, God did not hand His people a map. He gave them a cloud. A visible sign that He was near, moving, and trustworthy. The journey forward began not with certainty, but with Presence.

This first part lays the foundation for everything that follows. It invites you to lift your eyes, not to search for answers, but to recognize the God who still leads. You will see how He reveals Himself, how He draws near, how His voice cuts through confusion, and why delays and detours are often part of His design.

Trust does not start with knowing where you are going.

It starts with knowing who goes first.

CHAPTER 1

FOLLOW THE CLOUD

Trust Begins with God's Guiding Presence

*"By day the Lord went ahead of them in a pillar of cloud...
to guide them on their way."*

— EXODUS 13:21

God goes before us, and His presence leads the way.

The Pillar Cloud Appears

The desert presses in on you. Heat bears down like a weight you can't shake. Sand swallows the horizon in every direction. Fear settles in your chest.

Behind you is Egypt. Chains, bricks, Pharaoh's rage. You can still hear the crack of the whip echo in your memory. That was yesterday.

Ahead of you? Nothing but wilderness. No roads. No GPS. No plan.

You've been set free, but freedom feels terrifying when you don't know where it's taking you.

And then you see it. At first, it looks like a storm. But storms wander and dissipate. This one rises. Tall. Fixed. Alive.

By day, it stands against the desert sky, shimmering in the sun and casting shade across a weary people. By night, it blazes from within — not lightning that flashes and fades, but a steady fire that refuses to go out.

It leads.

When the pillar cloud moved, they moved. When it stopped, they stopped.

Families packed their tents. Children gathered their things. Leaders waited for the signal. The whole nation lived by its rhythm.

Each morning began with the same question: *Is the cloud rising, or is it staying?*

This is no ordinary cloud. This is the presence of God Himself. The God who brought you out. The God who goes ahead. The God who makes sure you are never alone in the wilderness.

The Heartbeat of This Book

This is both Israel's story—and ours.

God never designed you to figure life out alone. He wants to go with you.

He moves first. He leads.

The pillar of cloud in Exodus wasn't just a miracle for a wandering nation—it was a revelation of God's heart. A living picture of how He chooses to guide His people: not from a distance, not with blueprints, but with His presence. The same God who led Israel through deserts and dark nights is the God who longs to guide you—through your deserts, your delays, and your fog.

Here's the shift this book is calling you to make:

Look up instead of looking around.

Trust presence instead of plans.

When Israel followed the cloud, they discovered something life-changing—God's presence was better than certainty. Better than speed. Better than control.

He didn't give them the whole route in advance.

But He gave them Himself.

One step at a time.

One day at a time.

That's why I wrote this book—to walk with you into the real, everyday places of life. To help you stop chasing control and start trusting the God who still goes ahead of you.

My deepest "why" is simple: I want you to know what I've discovered. God doesn't merely show the way; He walks it with you. His presence is not abstract or distant; it is near, active, and personal. And it is the greatest gift you will ever receive.

What God promised Moses, He still promises His people today:

> **"My Presence will go with you, and I will give you rest."**
> **— Exodus 33:14**

That promise is the heartbeat of this book.

The Sky Speaks

Here's the thing — the pillar wasn't the first time God spoke through the sky. Long before Israel ever followed that cloud, He was already declaring His presence above. I love this bible verse.

> *"The heavens declare the glory of God."* — Psalm 19:1

I can picture David in those fields, forming the words he'd write by morning—leaning against a rock as his sheep settle around him. He looks up at a sky so vast it could swallow him whole, awed by the countless lights scattered across the moonless dark, each one whispering God's glory.

Centuries later, Paul said the same truth in different words:

> *"...since what may be known about God is plain... because God has made it plain. For since the creation of the world His invisible qualities—eternal power, divine nature—have been clearly seen, being understood from what has been made..."*— Romans 1:20

Before live-stream sermons. Before podcasts and Bible apps. God was already speaking. And He didn't start with preachers or prophets. He started with the sky.

Missing out on Hearing His Voice

But here's the problem: most of us barely look up anymore.

We keep our eyes down. Scroll. Swipe. Stuff the calendar and call it productivity. Then we lie in bed with that quiet ache — like something essential slipped through our fingers.

That ache isn't random.

It's God.

Stirring your spirit. Reminding you that you were made for more.

The writer and wise king once said,

"He has set eternity in the human heart." — Ecclesiastes 3:11

But we forget to look.

We bury eternity under busyness.

We fill silence with noise.

And then we wonder why God feels far away.

That's why He gave His people a cloud. Not a poem. Not a metaphor. A living sign saying: *I'm here. I'm leading. I'm ahead of you.*

God and Clouds in the Bible

Throughout Scripture, clouds are God's calling card — revealing His power, His presence, and His mystery. Track with me through the story.

At Mount Sinai, a thick cloud wrapped the mountain as God came to meet Moses (Exodus 19:9, 16–19). At Solomon's temple dedication, the glory-cloud filled the sanctuary until the priests couldn't even stand (1 Kings 8:10–11). Daniel saw "one like a Son of Man coming with the clouds of heaven" (Daniel 7:13). Prophets like Ezekiel and Joel warned of "a day of clouds" when God would judge, restore, and set things right.

The New Testament picks up the same thread — the transfiguration (Matthew 17:5), the ascension (Acts 1:9), and the promise of His return

(Revelation 1:7). In every moment, clouds both reveal and conceal — tangible signs of a God who is present, powerful, and near.

But the centerpiece is this: the pillar of cloud that led an entire nation out of slavery and into trust.

The Pillar Cloud That Led God's People
God Himself led the people of Israel.

> *"By day the Lord went ahead of them in a pillar of cloud to guide them on their way; by night in a pillar of fire to give them light… The cloud never left its place in front of the people."* — Exodus 13:21–22

This was no drifting mist. It was towering, lit from within, steady as stone. By day, it shimmered in the desert sun; by night, it burned like a torch, pushing back the dark.

And every morning, you'd step out of your tent and look up. The question wasn't, *What's my plan today?* The question was, *Is the cloud moving?*

If it rose, they packed up. If it stayed, they stayed. No timelines. No calendars. No illusion of control. God was calling them to trust.

And I'll be honest, something in me longs for that kind of simplicity. That ability to wake up, look up, and know exactly where God is leading.

Maybe you feel that too. A desire for a life shaped more by following than forcing. A life where presence, not pressure, sets the pace.

A Barrier of Protection

> *"The angel of God, who had been going ahead of Israel's camp, moved and went behind them; and the pillar of cloud shifted from in front of them and stood behind them…"* — Exodus 14:19–20

That night, the cloud was a shield. It stood between Israel and the Egyptian army. Darkness and confusion for the enemy. Light and protection for God's people.

The cloud protects.

He wasn't just leading from the front. He was guarding from behind. They were covered.

If I were preaching about this in one of my sermons, this is where I'd ask the audience to say it out loud and repeat after me: *God's got my back.*

When the Cloud Guided Me

Writing this book stirs more than Scripture. It stirs memories — and I've walked through seasons when I couldn't see two steps ahead, when God felt painfully silent. Times I was convinced I'd fallen short and disappointed Him… and wondered if maybe He wasn't with me anymore.

Maybe you've been there too — feeling lost, unsure, or questioning whether God is still guiding you.

Here's what I've learned: God's presence doesn't just comfort. Sometimes it redirects. Sometimes it interrupts.

One season I'll never forget came right after college.

I was back home, eager to make an impact in my hometown of Milwaukee. I longed to be used by God. I felt a pull, maybe even a calling, toward ministry. But the church leaders didn't see it. They told me I wasn't 'ministry material,' that others were better suited for the work. Those words cut deep, deeper than I let on. It felt like my future had been dismissed in a sentence.

It was more than their words; it was the weight behind them. In that moment, a fear I'd buried roared to the surface: Maybe I don't belong. Maybe I'll never measure up. Maybe my flaws and failures are too deep ever to overcome.

Discouragement set in. I felt drained. Spiritually dry. And then came the breaking point.

I was financially broke. My job barely covered rent. I had just walked through a painful breakup. And I was wrestling with private struggles I wasn't sharing with anyone.

One afternoon, I went on a prayer walk near downtown. The streets felt empty. I felt empty — invisible, as if I were watching my own life from the outside.

As I prayed, sorrow welled up inside. I was tired of pretending I was fine. Somewhere along the sidewalk, with tears in my eyes, I finally spoke honestly to God:

"God, I'm stuck. I'm not happy with where I am. I'm discouraged. I need You. I'm ready to get serious about following You — no more halfway. Help me."

There was no lightning bolt. No booming voice. But there was a sting of conviction mixed with a quiet assurance:

I'm here. I'm with you.

A Divine Appointment

I wiped my eyes and kept walking.

Somewhere deep inside, a thought surfaced: *I'm going to start being more active in sharing my faith.*

So I prayed — quick and simple: *Lord, lead me to someone who's looking for You.*

Minutes later, a guy about my age walked past. I stopped him. We talked. To my surprise, he was actually interested in God.

The next day, we met, opened the Bible, and not long after, he decided to follow Jesus. I got to see him baptized.

For him, it was joy. For me, it was something else.

It was God saying, "I got you." *I'm with you.*

Even when I felt like I didn't have what it takes.

Even when nobody else seemed to notice me.

Even when I was barely holding on to my own belief.

The Shift in My Soul

That encounter changed me.

The Spirit planted something inside — a quiet strength that began pushing the doubt out.

I stopped letting people define my calling.

I stopped living for their approval.

I stopped waiting for permission.

The version of me that played it safe didn't make it past that day.

If God could lead Israel with a cloud in the wilderness, He could lead me through the things wearing me down — the disappointments, the dead ends, the dry seasons. And He did.

God gave me confidence because His quiet impression on my soul reminded me He was with me — He always had been. I didn't need confirmation from some special victory. I just needed to believe.

Confidence. Yes. Godly confidence was poured into me that day.

What Happened Next

A year later, I was part of a church-planting team. Not long after, I was invited into full-time ministry — a door I didn't even know existed until God opened it.

That was more than 35 years ago. I'm still serving.

God pointed me to the right path and stayed with me.

And for me, it all started with a choice:

Look up.

Let go.

Follow.

He'll do the same for you.

So let me ask — where might God be calling you right now?

Out of the fog? Away from the map? Into something you can't yet see?

The wilderness is where I learned to listen. To trust. To follow.

My story isn't unique. Different city, different time, same God. Just as He trained Israel to live by His presence in the desert, He still trains us to trust one step at a time.

Eyes on the Cloud

Sometimes the cloud stayed overnight.

Sometimes for days.

Other times, months.

No calendars. No project timelines. No five-year plans. They lived by the cloud. It wasn't about speed or efficiency — it was about surrender.

"At the Lord's command they encamped, and at His command they set out… They obeyed the Lord's instructions, one day at a time."
— Numbers 9:18–23

Picture it. Before coffee. Before the commute. You glance up.

There it is — above the tabernacle. Steady.

Is it staying? Or starting to rise?

When it lifted, the trumpets sounded (Numbers 10:1–6).

One blast meant the leaders. Several blasts meant the whole camp. Suddenly, the place came alive. Tents came down. Families gathered their things. The tribes lined up, ready to follow.

Their rhythm was simple: Wait. Listen. Move.

Some days the cloud lifted quickly. Other times it hovered for weeks. And sometimes it didn't move at all.

When it rose, they rose. When it stayed, they stayed.

The living God was in their midst — setting the pace, choosing the road, guiding them step by step.

A Reflection for Us

That's what this book is really about.

Not trusting your plan, but trusting His presence.

Not looking ahead, but looking up.

Not moving first, but listening first.

The question is simple:

Are you ready to follow the cloud?

CLOUD MARKER

Control will fail you. Presence will lead you.

Prayer Prompt

Lord, I release my need to control what comes next.
Before I look ahead, I choose to look to You.
You go first — and I will follow, one step at a time. Amen.

Reflection Questions

1.   What would it look like this week if you truly trusted the cloud to lead you — even without a plan?
2.   Where have you been chasing control instead of staying close to God?
3.   Where might God be asking you to pause before you move?
4.   What is one clear step of faith He is asking you to take next?

Live It Out

Tomorrow morning, before the rush begins, pray:

Lord, where are You moving today — and how do You want me to follow?

Then stop.
Look up.
Listen.
And take the step He makes clear — even if it feels small.

CHAPTER 2

THE CLOUD BECAME FLESH

When the Presence Drew Near

"The Word became flesh and made his dwelling among us.
We have seen his glory, the glory of the one and only Son,
who came from the Father, full of grace and truth."

— JOHN 1:14

The cloud descended.

Where Was God?

There's a question many believers carry, but rarely say out loud—especially in church:

Where was God when I needed Him most?

Earlier in my faith, I wouldn't have admitted I wanted to ask that.

Not even to myself.

I had answers ready. Scriptures memorized.

A kind of religiosity that told me real faith didn't ask questions like this—it quoted verses instead of naming pain.

So, I learned how to keep the question buried.

But the question still lingered.

Where was God?

Not in a classroom debate.

Not in some late-night conversation about theology.

I mean when life knocked you flat.

When the pain was sharp.

When the silence swallowed your prayers.

Where was He…

…when the doctor spoke the word you feared?

…when the relationship that made you feel alive broke in your hands?

…when your prayers hit the ceiling, and silence answered back?

…when you buried a loved one too soon?

…when the paycheck stopped, and the pink slip came?

…when the people you trusted in church cut the deepest wound?

The truth is, you still believe in God—but He doesn't feel close.

You still say He's good—but you can't see it right now.

And the verses you underlined in your Bible about Him being *with you*? They don't land.

Right now, it feels like you're on your own.

It can feel risky to admit that.

As if naming the question might expose a weakness you were trained to hide.

But this isn't a skeptic's question.

It's a **wilderness question**—the cry of someone who wants to trust but can't get belief to line up with experience.

And you're not alone.

God's people have stood here before.

Freed from Egypt but still far from the promise, with sand in their shoes and fear in their bones, Israel wondered if God would still show up tomorrow—even with a pillar of cloud rising ahead of them.

And the way God answered them wasn't with distance—but with presence.

They kept looking up there, never realizing He was already on His way down here.

We make the same mistake.

Here's what I've learned: God's presence isn't found in having every answer. It's found in a Person. You see, the cloud didn't vanish. The Presence didn't hover in the heavens.

The cloud came down.

And then that cloud …

He put on skin.

He walked our roads.

He felt our hunger.

He faced our temptations.

He wept our tears.

The God who once led from the cloud now moves among us in flesh.

And once that truth breaks through, it reorders everything.

You stop scanning the sky, desperate for proof.

You start seeing the Savior who already stands with you.

Because the God beyond us has come near.

Emmanuel.

We Saw What Had Always Been There

I'll never forget the night it hit me.

A group of us from church — all city guys — decided to go camping in the Shenandoah Mountains. Most of us had never unplugged like that before. Honestly, a few were nervous. Bears were out there. And yes — we saw some. But no one got eaten, so we counted it a win.

That first night we pitched our tents, built a fire, and sat in the quiet. Then we looked up.

We froze.

The sky was clear. And more than that, it was alive.

The Milky Way stretched across the darkness like a silver highway. Dense. Radiant. Like God had spilled diamonds across black velvet. Some of the guys had never seen anything like it.

But here's the truth — those stars weren't new.

They'd been there all along.

We just had to get far enough from the glow of the city to finally see them.

That's what the Incarnation is like.

Jesus didn't suddenly appear out of nowhere.

He came into view.

What had always been near became unmistakably present.

He broke through the noise.

Cut through the static.

Slipped past the haze of religion and the glare of culture.

Not with fanfare.

With flesh.

He's always been here — present, faithful, radiant.

But our vision gets clouded.

We scroll past Him.

We run too fast to notice His voice.

We mistake His nearness for absence.

And then, one day, the noise quiets.

The distractions fall away.

Your eyes adjust.

And you realize: this isn't something new.

It's what was always there.

The God you thought had left — never left.

Not just watching.

Not just waiting.

With you.

Walking beside you.

Still.

The Journey of the Cloud

In the Old Testament, God didn't simply give His people commandments — He gave them **His presence**.

A visible sign of His invisible faithfulness.

"By day the Lord went ahead of them in a pillar of cloud to guide them..." — Exodus 13:21

It was more than a divine GPS. It was a statement of relationship:
"I am with you. I will go before you. Trust Me."
The cloud told Israel when to move, when to wait, and when to rest.
But more than that, it taught them this:
God was not just sending them somewhere — He was going with them.
And yet, even that cloud was a shadow of something greater to come.
Behind the cloud was not just a mysterious force… but a Person.
And that Person would one day take on flesh and walk among us.

Before the Cloud, there was a Flame in the Bush

Before God led Israel through the wilderness in a pillar of cloud, He first revealed Himself in a far more intimate and electrifying way — through a burning bush in the wilderness of Midian.

If you've seen the classic Charlton Heston *Ten Commandments* film, you remember the scene. But what Scripture describes is even more awe-striking than Hollywood could capture.

There, in the silence of a shepherd's ordinary day, God broke in.
He called Moses by name:
"Moses! Moses!"
And Moses replied, *"Here I am."*
Then came the words that set the tone for the entire story of redemption:

"Do not come any closer… Take off your sandals, for the place where you are standing is holy ground." — Exodus 3:4–5

In that holy conversation, Moses dared to ask what no one had asked before:

"If I go to the Israelites and tell them 'The God of your fathers has sent me,' and they ask, 'What is his name?' — what shall I say?"

And God spoke a name that still shakes the universe:

"I AM WHO I AM." — Exodus 3:13–14

In Hebrew, the word is *Ehyeh* — meaning *I AM* or *I WILL BE.*
It wasn't a riddle.
It was a revelation.
A declaration of His nature:
Unchanging.
Ever-present.
Always faithful.
The God who doesn't fade with time or shift with circumstance.
Then God gave Moses another name to carry to the people, a name built from the same root: Yahweh.
When God speaks of Himself, He says, **Ehyeh — "I AM."**
When we speak of Him, we say, **Yahweh — "HE IS."**
Together, these names echo through every generation, proclaiming:
He was.
He is.
He always will be.
The one Creator God — personal, present, eternal, and unmovable.
Only after this fiery bush encounter, after the trembling obedience, the ten plagues, the Passover night, and blood-stained doorposts — did Israel meet Yahweh in a new way: **as the pillar of cloud.**
The cloud was glorious, awe-inspiring, unmistakably divine. But it was never just a sign.
It was the presence of the same God who spoke from the flames.
The same "I AM" who called Moses by name.
The same faithful God who promised to be with His people step by step.
And He has not changed.
The God of the burning bush is the God of the pillar cloud.

And He is still the God who calls us by name today.

Yahweh, Our Heavenly Father

In the Old Testament, Yahweh was never a distant force in the sky. He revealed Himself as the personal Father.

"You, O Lord, are our Father..." — Isaiah 63:16

"Is not he your father, who created you...?" — Deuteronomy 32:6

These weren't poetic metaphors. They were reminders:
You belong. You're seen. You're His.
Then Jesus stepped onto the scene. And He didn't just *teach* this truth, He embodied it. He spoke of **"My Father"** with an intimacy that startled people.

"My Father is always at his work..." — John 5:17

"I and the Father are one." — John 10:30

For Jesus, "Father" wasn't a religious title; it was a reality of eternal relationship. In Him, Yahweh's heart was unveiled. Through Christ, we don't just learn about God, we meet a Father who knows us, delights in us, and calls us His own.

A Father We Can Trust

For many of us, the word *father* carries weight — sometimes wounds. Even the best dads are only shadows of the real thing. But in Jesus, we finally see the Father as He truly is:
The One who runs to the prodigal,
who counts the hairs on your head,
who loves without hesitation or condition.
This is why Jesus taught us to pray with two simple words: **Our Father.** Not "Cosmic Ruler." Not "Distant Sovereign." Father — personal, intimate, trustworthy.

The God Most High is your Father, and His love is steady, deep, and forever.

But the I AM WHO I AM wasn't revealed only as Father — He is also revealed fully in **the Son.**

Yahweh, the Son

We often think of Yahweh — God's covenant name — as referring only to the Father.

But read Scripture with open eyes, and a mystery unfolds:

The very titles, actions, and attributes of Yahweh are revealed fully in Jesus.

Then Jesus spoke the line that changed everything:

"Before Abraham was born, I AM." — John 8:58

This was no poetic flourish. It was a direct claim to divinity — a clear echo back to the burning bush in Exodus 3:14, where God declared His name: Ehyeh — I AM.

The religious leaders didn't miss it. That's why they reached for stones.

In their eyes, Jesus wasn't claiming to be close to God —

He was claiming to be God.

And this wasn't an isolated moment.

"I and the Father are one." — John 10:30

Again, stones in their hands.

"We are not stoning you for any good work," they said, *"but… because you, a mere man, claim to be God."* — John 10:33

They understood exactly what He meant — they simply refused to believe it.

The idea that Yahweh could stand before them in flesh felt unthinkable. Impossible.

But for believers, this is the cornerstone of our faith.
Jesus isn't merely a wise teacher or a miracle worker.
He is — and always has been — **the great I AM**:
the One who spoke from the bush,
who led in the cloud,
who holds the stars in place,
and who holds your story in His hands even now.

Not Just a Way to God — God on the Way to Us

The first Gospel written, Mark, doesn't warm up slowly. It opens with a bold announcement:

"I will send my messenger ahead of you… a voice of one calling in the wilderness, 'Prepare the way for the Lord.'" — Mark 1:1–3

Mark is tying together two Old Testament prophecies:

1. **Malachi 3:1** — God says He will send a messenger to prepare the way *before Him.*
2. **Isaiah 40:3** — A voice cries out, *"Prepare the way for the **LORD**."*

Here's the key:
In Isaiah, **"LORD" (in all caps)** is **Yahweh** — God's personal, covenant name.
Isaiah wasn't saying, "Someone is coming."
He was saying, **"God Himself is coming. Get ready."**
Now return to Mark.
Mark points to John the Baptist and says:
The messenger in Malachi? That was **John.**
The LORD in Isaiah who was coming? That is **Jesus.**
Mark is making a stunning claim:

Jesus isn't merely someone who shows us the way to God.

No. Jesus is not the Father — *but He is Yahweh*, coming toward us in human flesh.

So, when Mark writes, "Prepare the way for the Lord," he's not giving a slogan.

He is announcing:

The God of Creation has arrived.

He is here in person.

And His name is Jesus.

He hasn't just come to point out the path.

He is Yahweh in the flesh — and He has come for you, to bring you to the Father.

Mark introduces his gospel account saying: *This is the good news about Jesus the Messiah, the Son of God.*

This good news is the heartbeat of the whole Bible.

The God who once spoke from the mountain and led His people through deserts and seas now steps into *your* wilderness, opens a path where there wasn't one, and brings freedom and salvation right where you are.

The promised Presence isn't distant.

He came for you.

He came for me.

Christ in the Cloud

Contrary to what most people assume, Jesus doesn't first appear in the New Testament.

The Scripture tells a bigger story.

From the beginning, Christ was there — active, present, and leading His people.

It was Christ who went ahead of Israel in the cloud.

It was Christ who brought water from the rock.

And in the fullness of time, it was Christ who carried the cross and rose again.

Paul says it openly:

"They drank from the spiritual rock that accompanied them, and that rock was Christ." — 1 Corinthians 10:4

Jude says the same thing in some early manuscripts:

"Jesus… who saved a people out of the land of Egypt." — Jude 5 (ESV)

Early Christian writers preserved this reading, making clear that Jesus Himself was the one who delivered Israel.

Think about that.

The Jesus who healed the sick and walked the shores of Galilee
is the same God who split the Red Sea.
The One Israel followed in the cloud
is the same One we now follow in person.

"By day the LORD went ahead of them in a pillar of cloud…"
— Exodus 13:21

To put it simply:
The Rock was Christ.
The Deliverer was Christ.
The Cloud was Christ.
The same Presence who led them then
is the same Presence leading us now.

The Lord Was Always Here

"In the beginning was the Word, and the Word was with God, and the Word was God… Through him all things were made." — John 1:1–3

"The Word became flesh and made his dwelling among us." — John 1:14

The story of Jesus didn't begin in a manger, and His work didn't start at the cross. He has always been, and He will always be.

He pitched His tent among His people just like the tabernacle in the wilderness.

The story of God isn't about us climbing up to Him. It's about Him coming down to us.

So where is God when you need Him most?

He's not far. He came close.

You see, the God who goes before you also comes for you.

This means Jesus isn't just the way to God — He is God, on His way to you.

The Call to See Him

Maybe you're still not sure about all of this: about Jesus, about faith, about God coming close.

That's alright. You don't have to rush. Just stay open.

These first chapters are meant to give you something solid to stand on, a place to start, a foundation for the journey ahead.

But as you keep reading, I want to invite you to sit with a simple question:

What if God really did come close?

And, what if Jesus is exactly who He claimed to be?

You don't have to force yourself to believe it all at once.

Just begin noticing.

Pay attention.

Instead of scanning the sky for some dramatic sign, look at the quiet ways God may already be drawing near.

The stars were always there; you just needed to step away from the noise to see them.

Jesus has always been there, too. Maybe your eyes just haven't adjusted yet.

And when life feels silent, or the fog of doubt settles back in, here's what I remind myself:

He stepped into my story.

And if He came that far for me then, I can trust He's still here now.

And maybe — just maybe — He's closer to you than you think.

Look up. He hasn't left.

And He hasn't forgotten you, not for a moment.

My Prayer for You

That you won't just learn about Him but see Him.

That you'll recognize the same Jesus —

the One in the cloud,

the One who pitched His tent among us,

the One still walking beside you today.

And when you do, you'll stop asking, *"Where were You?"* and start saying, through tears, *"You were here all along."*

Always present.

Always near.

Always God.

The One in the cloud became flesh.

He didn't stay far.

He came close.

He came for you.

But seeing Him is only the beginning.

The question now is whether you'll follow His lead.

That's where we turn next — to the Guide you can't ignore.

CLOUD MARKER

The cloud didn't disappear—it descended.

Prayer Prompt

Lord, I've searched the sky and strained to feel You near. But You weren't far. You walked toward me. You bore my pain. You shared my dust. And now You walk with me still. Open my eyes to see You — not as absent, but as always present. The great "I AM," here and now.

Reflection Questions

1. Have I ever mistaken God's closeness for His absence?
2. How does knowing Jesus is the eternal "I AM" change the way I see the Old Testament?
3. What is one area of my life where I need to say, "You are here, and I will follow"?

Live It Out

This week, set aside time to sit in quiet — away from distractions — and read John 1:14 and Exodus 13:21–22 slowly. Don't just study them. Sit with them. Ask Jesus to show you where He's been walking with you all along — even when you didn't see Him.

Then write down one moment in your life where you now realize: "He was there."

Keep it as a reminder. Let it anchor your trust the next time the silence comes. Let His presence become your next step.

CHAPTER 3

THE VOICE IN THE FIRE

One Voice. One Fire. One Guide.

"Then a voice came from the cloud, saying, 'This is my Son, whom I have chosen; listen to him.'"

— LUKE 9:35

Many voices call. Only one leads home.

The Mountain and the Fire

It was supposed to be another climb. Another step into the wilderness. Moses had seen seas split and empires collapse. He had watched Pharaoh fall. But nothing could prepare him for Sinai.

The mountain shook. Smoke rose like a crown. Thunder cracked like war hammers against stone, echoing off the valley walls. Fire consumed the peak.

The people fell on their faces, pleading in terror: *"Do not let God speak to us directly, or we will die!"* — Exodus 20:19.

And then — the voice came.

Not thunder. Not earthquake. Not fire.

The voice of Yahweh. Commanding. Covenant-making. Carving history, shaking nations, engraving His name on stone and soul alike.

From that day, Israel was no longer just following a cloud. They were following a voice. A voice that roared from fire, proclaimed through prophets, burned in the scrolls, and one day took on flesh and said: "Come, follow me."

The story of Scripture is not humanity's search for God. It is the story of the God who descends, who burns, who speaks.

Yahweh — the God Who Speaks

In chapter two, we saw that both the eternal Father and the eternal Son are revealed as Yahweh. But Scripture is just as clear: the Spirit is Yahweh as well. The same Spirit who led Israel through the wilderness was not separate from the Father and the Son but one with them.

Isaiah leaves no room for doubt:

"They rebelled and grieved his Holy Spirit... yet they were given rest by the Spirit of the LORD. This is how you guided your people to make for yourself a glorious name." — Isaiah 63:10,14.

The Spirit did not merely symbolize God's presence; He is God's presence. The same Yahweh who called Moses from the burning bush, who descended in fire at Sinai, and who walked on the waves of Galilee was the very One who guided His people in the cloud.

The voice that speaks is not vague or generic. He is Yahweh — the LORD, the eternal, self-existent God. Scripture leaves no ambiguity: the Father is Yahweh (Isaiah 64:8; John 17:3). The Son is Yahweh (John 1:1; John 8:58; Hebrews 1:10). The Spirit is Yahweh (Isaiah 63:10–14; Acts 5:3–4; 2 Corinthians 3:17).

One God. Father. Son. Holy Spirit. One voice.

And because the Spirit is Yahweh, His voice is not secondary or optional — it is the very voice of God, guiding, convicting, and leading His people still today.

The Spirit of Christ Is the Holy Spirit

If the Spirit is Yahweh, then we have to ask: how does this connect to Jesus? The New Testament gives a clear and consistent answer — the Spirit who guided Israel is the very Spirit of Christ.

Paul makes it unmistakable:

- Romans 8:9–10 — *"the Spirit of God," "the Spirit of Christ,"* and *"Christ in you"* are used interchangeably.
- 1 Peter 1:11 — the prophets spoke by *"the Spirit of Christ"* who was working in them.
- Acts 16:6–7 — Luke refers to "the Holy Spirit" and *"the Spirit of Jesus"* as one and the same.

The Spirit of Christ is the Holy Spirit. Not two different spirits. Not competing voices. But one Spirit — eternally of God, sent by Christ, glorifying Christ, and uniting us to Christ.

To be Spirit-filled, then, is to be Christ-centered. To have the Spirit dwelling in you is to have Christ Himself living in you.

And this changes how we hear Him: the voice of the Spirit is the voice of Christ. The same Jesus who calmed storms and called disciples now speaks by His Spirit, guiding us through the noise of every other voice.

Christ-Followers, Spirit-Guided

This is why the Bible never separates discipleship into two tracks.

We are followers of Jesus — called to deny ourselves, take up our cross, and follow Him — Luke 9:23.

And we are led by the Spirit — *"For those who are led by the Spirit of God are children of God"* — Romans 8:14.

These are not two different callings. They are one reality.

To follow Christ is to be Spirit-guided.

To walk in the Spirit is to follow Christ.

And this is why the writer of Hebrews presses the same invitation again and again: *"Today, if you hear his voice, do not harden your hearts"* — Hebrews 4:7. God's call is never confined to the past. *"Today"* is always His word to us. Every moment becomes an opportunity to listen, to trust, to respond. Discipleship is not yesterday's obedience or tomorrow's intention — it is hearing His voice *today* and softening our hearts to follow where He leads.

And I will never forget how the Spirit's voice cut through the noise and spoke to my heart at a critical time in the history of our congregation.

A Moment When the Spirit Cut Through the Noise

One of the defining moments in my life — and in the life of our church family — came in the early 2000s.

As we became an independent, locally led congregation, God was clearly leading us forward in His purpose while gently guiding us away from a version of faith shaped more by people than by God's presence. We found ourselves at a crossroads: would we move with the shifting voices around us, or would we tune our ears to the Spirit of God?

As a leadership team, we committed ourselves to pray — not to defend, not to debate, but to listen. We wanted to follow the Spirit's lead, not the noise of the moment.

One early morning, while praying for direction and studying the book of Exodus, the Lord impressed a phrase on my heart so clearly it felt almost audible:

"Don't be afraid. Follow the cloud, not the crowd. Trust Me to guide you."

I sat with those words — not in fear, but in a deep sense of assurance and peace.

I shared them with my wife; she said, "Yes — that's God's word."

I shared them with my closest brothers; they felt the same conviction.

So I preached that message — *"Follow the Cloud, Not the Crowd"* — to our church.

As a young congregation, we committed to seeking God's voice above all others as we stepped into the future He was opening before us.

It wasn't a criticism of anyone.

It wasn't a reaction to circumstances.

It was a call to do what God's people have always been invited to do:

Listen for the One voice that still leads through the wilderness.

Months later, I was invited to preach a keynote message at an International Campus Ministry Conference in San Antonio in 2005. The sermon title was the same — *Follow the Cloud, Not the Crowd.* To the glory of God, the message steadied many hearts and reminded us all that even in confusing seasons, God's guidance never changes. Our task was — and still is — to trust His lead.

The Spirit and the Scriptures

Today, God's Spirit still speaks to those who quiet themselves long enough to listen.

But that raises an important question:

So how do we actually tune our ears to His voice?

We begin where God has always spoken — in the Word He breathed out.

Here's the danger: some claim, *"I'm following the Spirit,"* but ignore the very Scriptures the Spirit inspired. Others insist, *"I follow the Bible,"* but live as though the Spirit were silent, treating faith as a set of ancient rules instead of a living relationship with God.

Both are wrong. Both miss the point.

The Spirit and the Scriptures are not rivals. They are inseparably bound.

The Spirit is the breath that gave us the Word,

the voice that speaks through the Word,

and the power that applies the Word.

To separate them is to cut the living Word in half.

The Spirit inspired Scripture.

"All Scripture is God-breathed" — 2 Timothy 3:16. The word "breathed" is the language of Spirit. Every line of the Bible is alive because the Spirit

carried men along as they wrote (2 Peter 1:21). The Bible isn't just human reflection about God; it is God's own speech through the Spirit.

The Spirit illuminates Scripture.

"We have received… the Spirit who is from God, that we may understand what God has freely given us" — 1 Corinthians 2:12. Without the Spirit, the Bible can feel like words on a page. With the Spirit, the words pierce, awaken, and burn within us like they did for the disciples on the Emmaus road.

The Spirit confirms Scripture.

"The Holy Spirit also testifies to us about this…" — Hebrews 10:15–16, quoting Jeremiah. Every time you read the Word and feel its truth land deep — that's not just intellect, that's the Spirit testifying that this Word is God's Word. He doesn't just leave you with ink on parchment; He presses it into your soul.

The Spirit applies Scripture.

Paul calls the Word *"the sword of the Spirit"* — Ephesians 6:17. A sword in the hand of a warrior is no decoration — it's a weapon. The Spirit wields the Word to convict sin, to cut through lies, to defend against temptation, to build courage, and to shape us into Christ's likeness.

So yes — the Spirit still speaks today. But He speaks through the Word He breathed out. The Spirit never contradicts Scripture, never bypasses Scripture, never competes with Scripture. He is the voice within the Word, the breath behind the Word, the fire that makes the Word burn in your bones.

To ignore the Spirit is to read the Bible as though God were absent.

To ignore the Scriptures is to follow a spirit of your own imagination.

But to hold them together is to hear the living God.

Does the Spirit Still Speak Without Scripture?

Yes — but always with guardrails.

The book of Acts shows again and again that the Spirit is not silent. He spoke not only in general truths but in specific directions:

- *"Go to that chariot and stay near it."* — Acts 8:29
- *"Three men are looking for you. Get up and go downstairs."* — Acts 10:19–20
- *"The Spirit of Jesus would not allow them to enter Bithynia."* — Acts 16:7

These were not new doctrines or additions to Scripture. They were **situational promptings** that applied God's unchanging mission in a fresh moment.

The Spirit still works this way now.

He nudges. He convicts. He directs.

Sometimes it's a burden to pray for someone.

Sometimes it's courage to step through an open door — or restraint to walk away from a harmful one.

Sometimes it's the still, small whisper: *"This is the way; walk in it."*

Sometimes it's the power to forgive or the strength to break free from a familiar chain.

But here is the critical guardrail: **the Spirit never contradicts what He has already revealed.**

Paul warns, *"Even if we or an angel from heaven should preach a gospel other than the one we preached…"* — Galatians 1:8.

John commands, *"Test the spirits…"* — 1 John 4:1.

So yes — the Spirit still speaks, but not by adding new doctrines or alternate gospels.

His role is not to rewrite the Word but to **apply** it — pressing the presence of Christ into the details of your story.

Think of it this way:

Scripture is the map.

The Spirit is the Guide.

The Guide will never contradict the map — but He will show you the next step, when to wait, and when to move.

That is how the Spirit speaks today:

Not as a rival voice, but as the living voice of God who brings Christ near in every moment.

The Spirit Points to Christ

This is the anchor of everything we've said. Miss this, and you miss the Spirit's work.

Jesus promised it plainly:

"He will testify about me." — John 15:26

"He will glorify me…" — John 16:14

The Spirit does not spotlight Himself; He magnifies Jesus.

That's why Paul writes, *"No one can say, 'Jesus is Lord,' except by the Holy Spirit"* — 1 Corinthians 12:3. Every true confession, every step of obedience, every cry of surrender is evidence of His work.

You can trace this pattern through Scripture:

- **Sinai:** the cloud came with fire and a voice, calling Israel to obey God.
- **The Transfiguration:** the cloud overshadowed the mountain, and the voice declared, "This is my Son… listen to him."
- **Pentecost:** the Spirit came as fire, and the apostles exalted Christ: "God has made this Jesus… both Lord and Messiah."

The Spirit's role is consistent: **He points to Christ.**

This matters because many confuse spirituality with the Spirit. They chase experiences or feelings — but if it doesn't lead to deeper love for Christ, clearer vision of Christ, and fuller obedience to Christ, it isn't the Spirit.

Think of a floodlight at night. Its beam is real, but its purpose is to illuminate the building, not itself. You don't stare at the bulb; you see what it reveals. That is the Spirit. He whispers, "Don't look at me. Look at Him."

So ask yourself:

Am I seeing Christ more clearly?

Am I loving Him more deeply?

Am I following Him more closely?

If so, the Spirit is at work.

The Spirit points to Christ. He always has. He always will.

So, I Should Follow…?

If the Spirit points to Christ, and Christ points to the Father — who am I supposed to follow?

The answer is yes.

When you follow Jesus, you are following the Father.

When you listen to the Spirit, you are hearing Jesus.

They are not competing voices. They are the same voice.

"I and the Father are one." — John 10:30

"When the Spirit of truth comes, he will guide you into all truth… He will glorify me." — John 16:13–14

The Father sends the Son.

The Son sends the Spirit.

The Spirit leads us back to the Son.

And the Son brings us to the Father.

One unbroken circle of love. One eternal voice.

So you don't need to wonder who you're following.

When you tune your ear to Jesus, you are tuning into the voice of God Himself —

the same voice that spoke light into creation,

thundered on Sinai,

whispered to Elijah,

stilled the storm,

and called your name when you first believed.

That same voice still calls you now.

The Fruit of the Spirit

So how do you know if you're really listening to that voice? How can you tell if you're following the cloud or just following yourself?

Paul gives the test:

> *"The fruit of the Spirit is love, joy, peace, patience, kindness, goodness, faithfulness, gentleness, and self-control."* — Galatians 5:22–23

Fruit isn't forced. Grapevines don't strain to produce grapes. They simply abide, and fruit happens. In the same way, the fruit of the Spirit isn't the product of willpower, but the overflow of a life surrendered to His guidance (John 15:5).

Love that gives.

Joy that endures.

Peace in the storm.

Patience that holds.

Kindness and goodness that reflect God's compassion.

Faithfulness that stands.

Gentleness that restrains.

Self-control that frees.

This isn't a buffet to pick and choose. Paul doesn't say fruits (plural). He says fruit (singular). One harvest. One life. One transformation into Christ's likeness.

You cannot claim to be Spirit-led and stay spiritually stagnant.

You cannot call yourself a follower of Jesus and refuse to grow in love — especially toward the people who stretch you the most.

You cannot say you're following the cloud while knowingly sowing anger, envy, division, or selfish ambition into your relationships.

The Spirit guides you toward a destination and even deeper into a transformation.

The power and presence of God is forming someone in you — someone who looks like, loves like, and lives like Jesus.

So, Who Are You Listening To?

Who really has your ear?

The crowd shouts.

The culture seduces.

And your own restless heart echoes with doubt and desire.

But through it all, there has always been one voice.

At Sinai, the mountain convulsed, fire split the sky, and the cloud descended. The people trembled, but one truth rang clear: only one voice mattered.

At the Transfiguration, the cloud overshadowed the mountain, and heaven thundered: *"This is my Son… listen to him."*

At Pentecost, fire rested on every head, and every tongue declared the same Name: Jesus.

Only one voice cuts through the storm.

Only one voice has the power to transform.

Only one voice leads home.

And that voice has not gone silent. The Spirit still guides, convicts, and presses Christ into your very story. But mark this: He will always point you to Jesus.

To follow the cloud is to follow the Spirit.

To follow the Spirit is to listen to the Son.

To listen to the Son is to hear the Father.

One Guide you cannot ignore.

The same fire that shook the mountain,

the same fire that fell at Pentecost,

if you are a cloud follower, now burns within you — calling, convicting, consuming.

The invitation that steadied my steps remains unchanged: follow the cloud, not the crowd.

Let Him lead you. Listen — and live.

CLOUD MARKER

**The Spirit's voice is the cloud's movement —
and He always leads you to Christ.**

Prayer Prompt

Spirit of the living God, quiet the noise within me and around me.

Tune my heart to the voice of Jesus.

I choose to follow Him — not the crowd, not my fears, not competing voices.

Lead me step by step, and give me courage to obey what You show me. Amen.

Reflection Questions

1. Where are you most tempted to listen to competing voices instead of Christ?
2. How have you seen the Spirit guide God's people in Scripture — and in your own story?
3. Why is it vital that the Spirit of Christ and the Holy Spirit are one and the same?
4. What will it look like in your daily life to keep Scripture and the Spirit inseparably together?
5. What step of faith is the Spirit pressing on your heart right now?

Live It Out

Choose one passage of Scripture this week — for example, **John 10:1–18** (the Shepherd's voice). Read it slowly three times. With each reading, pause and ask:

1. *Spirit, what do You want me to see?*
2. *Spirit, what do You want me to understand and take to heart?*
3. *Spirit, what do You want me to do?*

Then write down **one clear action** that flows from what you've seen.

Take that step this week — trusting the Spirit to guide you as you follow Christ.

CHAPTER 4

THE SCENIC ROUTE

God Uses the Long Way to Prepare us for the Promise

*"When Pharaoh let the people go, God did not lead them
on the road through the Philistine country, though
that was shorter... So God led the people around
by the desert road toward the Red Sea."*

— EXODUS 13:17–18

The shortest path isn't always the one that forms us.

The Scenic Route: Slower, Longer, But Worth It

When you're in a hurry, God rarely is.

He's not rushing to get you somewhere — He's shaping who you'll be when you arrive.

We want answers yesterday, breakthrough today, and arrival tomorrow.

But sometimes, God says:

"Not yet. Not that way. Follow Me instead."

And the route He takes?

Winding. Delayed. Frustrating. Scenic.

It doesn't feel spiritual. It just feels slow.

But make no mistake — it isn't a waste.

It's where God works.

The Lie We Believe on the Long Road

Here's the lie that creeps in when the road stretches longer than we thought:

"If this were really God's plan, I'd be there by now."

We don't always say it out loud, but we feel it.

When progress is slow, we assume something's wrong.

Either we must have missed God's will… or God is holding out on us.

We start comparing our pace to others.

We start wondering if we should take matters into our own hands.

We start treating delays as proof that God has gone quiet—or worse, absent.

But that's not how He works.

The truth? God's timing is never late, never wasteful, and never careless.

"For my thoughts are not your thoughts,
 neither are your ways my ways,"
 declares the Lord.
"As the heavens are higher than the earth,
 so are my ways higher than your ways
 and my thoughts than your thoughts." — *Isaiah 55:8–9*

Underline this point: **God sees what you can't.**

He knows the dangers on the shorter road, the battles you're not ready for yet, the lessons you'd miss if you arrived too soon.

His delays are not denials—they're preparations.

It's protection.

It's formation.

It's the place where God grows trust that can't be shaken when you finally arrive.

So when the journey feels slow, don't rush to escape it.

Ask instead: *"Lord, what are You building in me here that I'll need when I get there?"*

A Story from the Road

I've asked that question more than once—especially on long drives that felt like they would never end.

Years ago, when our three boys were small, my wife Charon and I would pile everyone into the minivan for regular trips from Maryland to the Midwest to visit family. It was a circus on wheels — juice boxes, backpacks, graham crackers, a few battered Power Rangers, and always one too many bathroom stops.

Back then, we didn't have GPS. We had a crumpled paper road atlas in the glove box and a well-worn routine.

Most people took I-76 — faster, straighter, toll-heavy. I chose I-68 instead — longer, slower, but beautiful.

Rolling hills. Deep valleys. Open skies that made you pause.

It took more time, but it gave us something more valuable: space. Laughter. Rhythm. Connection.

Charon packed like a pro. And yes, she also ran the soundtrack. The boys had one request every trip: *Space Jam.*

That CD was our anthem. And yes — I can still sing it word for word.

But even with snacks, books, and music, the questions came:

"Are we there yet?"

"I'm hungry."

"How much longer?"

"He's breathing on me!"

If you've parented on a road trip, you get it.

If you've followed God on a longer-than-you-hoped journey, you get it too.

Because here's the truth:

The scenic route always takes longer.

But that doesn't mean it's wrong.

It means God is doing something deeper.

The Sea Wasn't a Setback — It Was the Setup

And just like those trips, Israel's scenic route ended at a place no one would have chosen — the edge of a sea.

You've just escaped slavery. You're finally free.

But now you're standing at the water's edge — trapped.

Behind you: Pharaoh's army, roaring toward you in a storm of dust and fury.

Before you: endless water. Deep. Cold. Impassable.

No way forward. No way back. No good options. Just fear.

The ground shakes beneath charging chariots.

Metal clinks. Horses snort.

People scream. Mothers cling to their children. Fathers freeze.

Some collapse. Some cry. Some curse.

And somewhere in the center of it all… the cloud — God's very presence — just hovers.

It led them here.

To this impossible place.

It made no sense.

This was supposed to be deliverance — not a death trap.

This was freedom?

This felt like a setup.

But before panic swallowed them whole, a voice cut through the chaos.

So the questions came:

- "Why here? Does God know where He is leading me?"
- "Why now? Does God know the stress I'm under?"
- "Why this route? Did God make a mistake?"

That's what fear does — it distorts.

It makes Egypt look better than the promise.

It makes slavery feel safer than surrender.

And just like kids in the back seat of a long road trip, their complaints spilled out fast:

"Are we there yet?"
"Why did we come this way?"
"We should've stayed where we were."
But in the chaos, one voice stood up.
Moses.
Steady. Clear. Unshaken.

"Do not be afraid.
Stand firm and you will see the deliverance the Lord will bring you today.
The Lord will fight for you; you need only to be still."
— Exodus 14:13–14

That wasn't just leadership — it was faith.
Because here's the truth they didn't yet see:
This wasn't a wrong turn. It was a divine setup.
God led them there on purpose.
Not to destroy them — but to deliver them in a way only He could.
This wasn't just about escape.
It was about trust.
It was about learning that when there's no human way forward, **God becomes the Way.**

Lessons from the Red Sea

Here's what that moment still teaches us:

1. God's Way Is Longer — But Always Purposeful

The shorter route wasn't safer. It was a setup for failure.

God saw what they couldn't: the enemies ahead, the weakness within, the trust that still had to be formed.

The long way was for their good.

"In their hearts humans plan their course, but the Lord establishes their steps." — Proverbs 16:9

If you're feeling stuck on a longer-than-expected journey, remember: God's delays are never random.

They're strategic. Protective. Formative.

You're not being punished. You're being prepared.

2. Fear Will Always Tempt You to Go Back

When trust feels risky, we crave what's familiar — even if it was slavery.

That's how Egypt starts to look good again.

In fear, our memories get distorted. We forget the chains and remember the comfort of predictability. We convince ourselves that the old life wasn't so bad — at least we knew what to expect. At least we could control it.

That's exactly what Israel did. With the Red Sea in front of them and Pharaoh's army behind them, they cried out, *"It would have been better for us to serve the Egyptians than to die in the desert!"* (Exodus 14:12).

Fear will always try to rewrite your history so you'll abandon your future.

But God's call is clear:

Don't go back. Don't retreat. Don't shrink.

"The Lord will fight for you; you need only to be still." — Exodus 14:14

Sometimes, the bravest thing you can do is stay put and trust.

Not push. Not plan. Not manipulate the outcome.

Just stand still — and believe.

Because here's the truth: the enemy chases hardest right before God parts the waters.

3. The Impossible Is God's Favorite Stage

To Israel, the Red Sea was the end.

They could smell the salt water in front of them and the dust from Pharaoh's chariots behind them. There was no human way forward — and no human way out. Every survival instinct screamed, *"This is it."*

But to God, that impossible moment was not the end — it was the perfect opening scene for His deliverance.

God has a pattern. Again and again in Scripture, He steps onto the stage when the lights are darkest and the script seems finished:

- **Abraham and Sarah's empty nursery** — He brings life from a barren womb (Genesis 21:1–2).
- **Gideon's outnumbered army** — He wins the battle with only 300 men (Judges 7:7).
- **Elijah on Mount Carmel** — He answers with fire on a soaked altar (1 Kings 18:36–38).
- **The disciples in the storm** — He commands the wind and waves with a word (Mark 4:39).
- **The sealed tomb in Jerusalem** — He rolls the stone away (Luke 24:1–6).

It's as if God waits until human resources are exhausted so there's no confusion about who gets the glory.

"What is impossible with man is possible with God." — Luke 18:27

That thing in your life right now that feels impossible?
That diagnosis.
That prodigal child.
That financial hole.
That call from God that seems too big for you.
That might be the exact stage God is setting to reveal His power.
He turns dead ends into doorways.
Barriers into breakthroughs.
Traps into testimonies.
When the impossible rises up before you, don't assume you've reached the end of the road.
It may be the place where God wants to write His most unforgettable scene in your story.

4. The Long Way Is the Forming Way

God wasn't just getting Israel to the Promised Land.

He was getting Egypt out of them.

They had walked out of Pharaoh's borders, but Pharaoh's mindset was still lodged in their hearts — the fear, the survival mentality, the reflex to trust human hands more than God's. Freedom on the outside means little if bondage still lives on the inside.

That kind of transformation takes time.

It can't be microwaved. It's slow-cooked in the wilderness.

The desert became their classroom. The manna and the cloud were their daily assignments. Trust wasn't a lecture they heard once; it was a habit they learned over miles and months. Every step on the long road chipped away at their slavery-shaped thinking and built a God-shaped trust.

"Let perseverance finish its work so that you may be mature and complete, not lacking anything." — James 1:4

That's what the scenic route does. It finishes the work.

It refuses to rush the process.

It gives God space to grow roots deep enough to hold when storms come.

We think God is only interested in getting us to the destination, but He is far more committed to the person we are becoming along the way. The Promised Land without a transformed heart would have been just another Egypt with new scenery.

So Don't Miss This

The Red Sea wasn't a failure of direction — it was a feature of formation.

God meant for them to be there.

And He means for you to be here too.

If you're stuck, stalled, afraid, or doubting… you might not be off-course.

You might be right where He does His best work.

The very place you're questioning might be the place He is shaping you most.

You might be on the edge of a miracle.

God didn't take the wrong route.

He's just not finished with yours yet.

Invitation to Reflect

These lessons aren't just for Israel at the Red Sea — they're for us today.

Where in your life do you feel stuck between an army and an ocean? Where are you questioning God's timing or direction?

Maybe you're in a season that feels longer than you imagined. Maybe fear is tempting you to run back to old comforts. Maybe you're facing something that looks impossible, and you can't see a way forward.

Pause and consider:

- Where might God be protecting you by taking you the long way?
- Where is He inviting you to stand firm rather than turn back?
- What "impossible" situation might become a stage for His faithfulness?
- How might He be shaping your trust and character more than simply rushing you to a finish line?

Oh... Now I See — God Was Taking Me the Scenic Route

Hindsight is a gift. So often, I only recognize God's fingerprints after the dust has settled.

And years later, I discovered the Red Sea wasn't just their story — it was mine too.

There was a stretch early in our ministry — five whirlwind years — when Charon and I moved seven times across four states. Each child arrived with a new address. Every move brought fresh friendships, sacred memories, and moments of ministry we'll always treasure... but raising a young family in constant transition was exhausting. I carried a weight I couldn't put down.

One season in particular tested us deeply. We served in a couple of churches that, over time, had drifted from keeping Christ at the center. Leaders were followed more like celebrities than servants. Tensions in leadership sprang less from a shared pursuit of God's will and more from ambition, image, and control. Broken relationships were left to fester. Moral failings were quietly ignored as long as charisma and results were delivered. But cracks like that never stay hidden forever.

It was painful to witness — and even harder to navigate. My wife and I kept asking: *How do we stay spiritually grounded in a system that rewards performance over transformation?*

Eventually, we knew we couldn't. I remember telling a mentor, "We're done." We weren't walking away from God — just from the chaos, to protect our hearts and our family.

Still, I wrestled: *Why this route, Lord? Why all of this?*

We prayed. We asked for directions. We made plans. And we waited.

A week later, the phone rang. An unexpected invitation came — a call to serve in a church in the Washington, DC area. It felt like a lifeline. Not because we suddenly had all the answers, but because we sensed God's voice saying, *"I'm still leading. Keep trusting. I'm not finished with you."*

So we packed up — again — and went. And we've been ministering in the DMV area ever since.

Looking back now, I see it clearly:

- Those closed doors? **Classrooms.**
- Those transitions? **Training grounds.**
- That chaos? **Preparation.**

God was revealing blind spots and weaknesses in my own heart — things I wouldn't have seen otherwise. He was pruning me, teaching me, and preparing me for challenges ahead. Through it all, He was leading me to depend more on Him and less on myself.

He was forming us. Stretching us. Building trust that could stand when everything else felt unstable.

The hard road wasn't a mistake.

It wasn't the wrong way.

It may have been the longer way.

Ultimately, it was the best way — God's scenic route.

The View from Here

If you had told me back then — in the middle of the chaos, the moves, and the questions — that I was on the right road, I'm not sure I would've believed you.

But standing here now, I can see it: the scenic route wasn't an accident. It was a mercy.

The same God who led Israel by cloud and fire was leading me, step by step. He knew what I didn't — the battles ahead, the pride that needed pruning, the trust that needed to grow deep enough to hold when everything else shook.

And here's what I know for certain:

God's road is never wasted.

Not a mile. Not a detour. Not a delay.

One day, you'll stand where I'm standing. The fog will clear, the questions will fade, and the very road you wanted to escape will be the one you thank Him for. You'll realize the long way wasn't just the best way — it was the only way to arrive whole.

So keep walking. Keep trusting. Keep following the cloud.

The One who brought you this far will see you safely home — in His time, by His way, for His glory.

CLOUD MARKER

**God's delays aren't detours —
they're invitations to deeper trust.**

Prayer Prompt

Father, I confess that I often want the fastest route, the clearest plan, and the quickest resolution.

But You see what I cannot.

Help me trust Your timing, Your path, and Your purpose—especially when the road winds longer than I expected.

Teach me to rest in Your presence rather than rush ahead of You.

Use this season to shape my heart, not just move me forward.

In Jesus' name, amen.

Reflection Questions

1. Where in your life are you experiencing a "scenic route"—a path that feels longer than you hoped or expected?
2. What fears or frustrations surface when God doesn't move as quickly as you want?
3. How has God used delays or detours in your past to grow your faith or form your character?
4. Is there an "Egypt" you feel tempted to return to—something familiar, but ultimately limiting or enslaving?
5. What would it look like to trust that the place where you feel stuck may actually be a setup for God's deliverance and glory?

Live It Out

Write a short prayer or journal entry naming the area of your life where you feel delayed, stuck, or confused right now.

Then read **Exodus 14:13–14** aloud—slowly and prayerfully.

As you read, ask God to help you:

- stand firm when fear rises,
- stay still when impatience presses in,
- and trust Him to fight for you—even when the way forward isn't clear.

PART TWO

WHEN FOLLOWING GETS HARD

FOLLOWING GOD IS simple—until it isn't.

There comes a moment in every journey when the cloud leads into places that feel uncomfortable, unclear, or costly. The noise grows louder. The pressure intensifies. The crowd pulls. And the question shifts from *Do I believe God leads? To Will, I keep following when it gets hard?*

This part explores what happens when trust is tested. When conviction collides with conformity. When faith requires community. When silence becomes necessary. When the fog rolls in and clarity disappears.

These chapters are not about perfection. They are about formation. About learning how God shapes His people in the middle of resistance, uncertainty, and waiting. Not by removing the pressure—but by meeting us in it.

Following was never meant to be easy.

But it was always meant to be shared—and sustained by God's presence.

CHAPTER 5

DON'T FOLLOW THE CROWD

Choosing Conviction Over Conformity When the Crowd Presses In

*"Do not conform to the pattern of this world,
but be transformed by the renewing of your mind."*

— ROMANS 12:2

You can't follow the cloud and follow
the crowd at the same time.

Safety in Numbers?

In the ocean, small fish rely on one main survival instinct: stick together.

When a predator shows up — maybe a shark's shadow or a sudden rush in the water — they don't scatter. Instead, they press closer, forming what scientists call a *bait ball*. From above, it looks like a single swirling silver mass, flickering and shifting as the fish move in frantic unison.

At first glance, this seems wise. Alone, a fish is an easy target. Together, they create a confusing blur, making it harder for a predator to lock onto just one. Scientists call this *predator confusion*, and in some cases, it works.

But here's the twist.

Predators know this instinct well, working together to exploit it. Dolphins and sharks herd the fish into a dense, trembling sphere, then take turns charging through — a shark slicing straight through the mass, leaving a trail of silver scales and empty space. Then it circles back while another moves in.

Above, seabirds dive to pick off fish near the surface. Below, larger fish wait for anything that tries to break free downward. Every escape route is covered.

Little by little, the ball shrinks. Each attack thins the group further, until what started as a swirling fortress becomes a shrinking, desperate shadow of itself. The fish tighten more, hoping to protect themselves, but the mass keeps getting smaller — until it's almost completely gone.

What looked like safety in numbers becomes an organized feast. The very instinct that promised protection ends up making them easy targets, each pass of a predator consuming more of the group until nothing remains.

We may not swim in salt water, but we know this instinct well.

When we feel threatened, insecure, or unsure, we press into the crowd. We tell ourselves that if we just stay close enough, blend in enough, we'll be safe. We think, *If I go along, I won't stand out. If I stay quiet, I won't get hurt.*

But the crowd won't save you. The crowd won't protect your soul. The crowd won't lead you to life — it only makes you more vulnerable to forces that want to shape you and slowly consume your convictions.

That's why this chapter matters. Because when the crowd presses in, it takes real courage to stand apart. To choose conviction over conformity. To step out of the swirling bait ball and follow the cloud of God's presence — even if it costs you approval.

We see this clearly in Scripture. Let's look at two moments where the crowd pressed in and God's people faced the choice: cave in, or stand firm.

That instinct to press in for safety didn't start in the ocean. God's people knew it well — and at Sinai, it nearly destroyed them.

When the Crowd Shapes Your Beliefs and Values
(The Golden Calf — Exodus 32)

The people of Israel had experienced God's presence in ways no generation before them ever had.

The cloud had led them out of Egypt—moving ahead by day, glowing like fire by night, guiding every step of their journey. It stopped when God stopped. It moved when God moved. Their lives were ordered around His presence.

At Sinai, the mountain shook. Thunder rolled. Lightning flashed. The cloud descended in terrifying power. They heard God's voice directly—not through a prophet—as He gave them the Ten Commandments. Trembling, they promised together, *"All that the Lord has spoken we will do, and we will be obedient"* (Exodus 24:7).

Then Moses went up the mountain.

Days stretched into weeks. *The cloud still hovered—but Moses disappeared into it.* Fear crept in. Patience wore thin. And when people feel exposed and uncertain, the crowd always wants a quicker, safer solution.

So they gathered around Aaron and said, *"Come, make us gods who will go before us. As for this fellow Moses… we don't know what has happened to him"* (Exodus 32:1).

The tragedy is hard to miss. One of God's very first commands had been clear:

"You shall not make for yourself an image… you shall not bow down to them or worship them" (Exodus 20:4–5).

Yet in the shadow of the mountain—while God was still speaking to Moses—they demanded an idol.

Aaron felt the pressure of proximity. Surrounded by anxious voices, he forgot the cloud that had led them and yielded to the crowd that was pressing him. He did not guide the people back to God; he allowed the people to guide him. Instead of calling them higher, he gave them what they craved.

He took their gold, melted it down, shaped it into a calf—something visible, manageable, controllable. Then he built an altar and declared a festival *"to the LORD,"* blending compromise with worship.

That day, Aaron wasn't just making an idol. He was surrendering conviction to the roar of the crowd.

The result was chaos—dancing, shouting, unrestrained worship that betrayed the very God who had delivered them. When Moses came down the mountain, he found a people who had chosen noise over presence, popularity over purity. Aaron's fear of losing the crowd nearly cost Israel their future with God.

This is why the old saying carries uncomfortable truth:

"You are the average of the five people you spend the most time with."

Whether or not the wording is precise, Scripture affirms the reality beneath it: *"Bad company corrupts good character"* — 1 Corinthians 15:33.

We may not melt gold into statues today, but we reshape our beliefs all the time. We soften truth to avoid tension. We stay silent to protect relationships. We adjust our view of God to match the room—smaller, safer, less demanding. Over time, the crowd doesn't just influence our behavior; it reforms our values and rewrites our theology.

When you live to please the crowd, you will always end up building idols.

And idols always cost more than you expect.

The danger of the crowd doesn't end with idols made of gold. Sometimes it looks far more respectable. Sometimes the crowd doesn't ask you to worship something false—it simply asks you to stay quiet about what's true.

In the wilderness, fear pushed Israel to reshape God into something manageable. In Jerusalem, fear pushed believers to shrink their faith into something private. The form changed, but the pressure didn't. When approval begins to matter more than obedience, silence becomes the new sacrifice—and truth is the first thing laid on the altar.

When Approval Matters More Than Truth
(John 12:42–43)

By the time Jesus entered Jerusalem, His miracles and teachings had shaken the entire region. Crowds gathered. The conversations and questions spread through homes, markets, and synagogues: *Could this be the Messiah?*

Even among the religious leaders — the insiders with the most to lose — belief began to take root. John records it plainly:

> *"Yet at the same time many even among the leaders believed in him. But because of the Pharisees they would not openly acknowledge their faith for fear they would be put out of the synagogue; for they loved human praise more than praise from God." — John 12:42–43*

They believed, but they stayed silent.

Why? Because the cost was high.

To be "put out of the synagogue" wasn't just skipping worship. It was losing your community. Your family could cut ties. Your reputation could collapse. Your livelihood could be stripped away. The synagogue wasn't just a building — it was belonging, identity, life. To lose it felt like losing yourself.

So they hid. They blended in. They tried to carry faith in their hearts while keeping their place in the crowd.

The Real Cost of Staying Silent

The leaders in John's Gospel weren't confused about Jesus. They saw the miracles, they knew the prophecies, they recognized the truth. **What they lacked was courage**.

And that same pressure lives on today.

- **Relational Pressure** — Many stay in religious or cult-like systems even after seeing the cracks, because leaving means losing family, friends, and support. Better to remain silent than be shunned.
- **Cultural Pressure** — Identity groups act like tribes. We feel forced to vote, speak, or act in lockstep — not out of conviction but out of loyalty.
- **Social Pressure** — On campuses, in workplaces, and online, mob mentality rules. People post or shout things they'd never say alone because the crowd gives them cover.

- **Psychological Pressure** — Fear of rejection is real. Studies show rejection lights up the same parts of the brain as physical pain. No wonder human approval feels like oxygen — and losing it feels like suffocating.

This is why conformity is so seductive.

When you cling to the crowd just to belong, you lose yourself. You water down truth to keep your place. You mold into their shape — even when you know it isn't truth but conformity.

And here's the tragedy: the belonging you grab for eventually shrinks you. Your voice grows faint. Your courage withers. Your calling gets buried under compromise until the person God made you to be is barely recognizable.

Jesus said it plainly: *"What good is it for someone to gain the whole world, yet forfeit their soul?"* (Mark 8:36).

Gain the crowd, lose your soul. Keep their praise, miss His presence.

That's what happened to the leaders in John 12. History doesn't remember them for wisdom, but for fear. John sums it up in one piercing line: *"They loved human praise more than praise from God."*

And that same danger hasn't disappeared. It shows up when someone dares to speak about sexual purity in a culture that shrugs at compromise. It shows up in politics, where movements demand loyalty and punish anyone who questions them. It shows up in conversations about identity, where holding to God's truth can cost you friends, respect, or even your livelihood. Different place, same pressure: the crowd rewards silence and punishes conviction.

The same choice stands before us still:

Stay silent — and keep the crowd.

Or speak up — and follow the cloud.

Only one leads to life.

And this isn't theory. I've seen it with my own eyes.

When the Crowd Costs You, Christ

I think of a friend I once helped introduce to Christ. He had grown up in the Watch Tower Society, known as Jehovah's Witnesses. For years, he followed their teachings — but he also carried a hunger to know God more personally.

We began studying the Scriptures together, week after week. Slowly, the truth came alive for him: that Jesus is not just a created being but both Lord and Christ — fully God and fully human — and that salvation is found in Him alone. He wrestled with it, counted the cost, and then did something I had rarely seen from someone inside that organization: he surrendered his life to Christ.

But the cost was immediate. His family and friends shunned him. Invitations stopped. Conversations ended. The very people who had been his world now turned their backs.

Months later, the weight became unbearable. The loneliness pressed harder than his convictions. And in the ache of wanting to stay close to his family, he laid down what he had once boldly embraced. He renounced who Jesus truly is and returned to the group.

That's the power of the crowd. It promises belonging, but at the cost of truth. And many, like my friend, face that impossible choice: stand firm and lose everything familiar, or conform and keep the crowd.

And it's not only religious groups that raise the cost. Sometimes it's friend groups. When someone begins to follow Christ, friends can feel threatened — as if your new convictions are a judgment on their old choices. Some drift away. Some mock. Others pressure you to return to old patterns so they don't feel left behind.

The pull of the crowd is real. But you can't keep the crowd and keep Christ at the same time.

And that's precisely why Scripture warns us again and again. God knows the power crowds have over our hearts, and He speaks clearly about the danger of trading truth for approval.

The Scriptures Are Clear

Exodus 23:2 — *"Do not follow the crowd in doing wrong."*

Psalm 1:1 — *"Blessed is the one who does not walk in step with the wicked or stand in the way that sinners take or sit in the company of mockers."*

Isaiah 51:7 — *"Hear me, you who know what is right, you people who have taken my instruction to heart: Do not fear the reproach of mere mortals or be terrified by their insults."*

Matthew 10:32–33 — *"Whoever acknowledges me before others, I will also acknowledge before my Father in heaven. But whoever disowns me before others, I will disown before my Father in heaven."*

Galatians 1:10 — *"Am I now trying to win the approval of human beings, or of God? Or am I trying to please people? If I were still trying to please people, I would not be a servant of Christ."*

God knows the power crowds have over us. He knows how easily we are swayed by approval, pressured by opinions, and tempted to trade truth for belonging. That's why His Word warns us again and again: don't follow the many, don't fear rejection, don't live for human praise. Instead, set your heart on Him.

The crowd may promise safety, but it cannot give you life. Only His presence can. That's why the choice is so clear: when the crowd presses in, follow the cloud.

Pressure of the Crowd

We don't grow out of peer pressure — it just changes shape.

As kids, it shows up on the playground or in the lunchroom. We learn early that standing out can cost us friends.

In high school, it looks like staying silent when someone crosses a line. In college, it might mean hiding your faith because it feels "unpopular." As adults, it gets sneakier — nodding along in meetings, ignoring convictions in business deals, or curating an online persona so no one can criticize us.

Peer pressure is powerful because we were created to belong. But when we start bending convictions to keep our seat at someone else's table, we trade true belonging for shallow applause.

And here's what makes it so dangerous: peer pressure doesn't just reshape behavior — it reshapes your mind. That's why Paul wrote, *"Do not conform to the pattern of this world, but be transformed by the renewing of your mind"* (Romans 12:2). If you're not intentionally renewing your mind with God's truth, the world will rewire it for you.

In the end, peer pressure is just another form of the bait ball instinct — pressing in for safety, blending in for survival. It feels easier in the moment, but it always costs more than we realize. Jesus never called us to blend in. He called us to stand out — to love deeply without surrendering truth, and to walk the narrow road even if it means walking alone.

Three Steps Toward Courage

Courage doesn't appear all at once. It grows slowly, one decision at a time. Here are three ways to take your next step out of the bait ball and into the cloud:

1. Examine Your Crowd

Ask yourself: Who has the loudest voice in my life right now?

Whose approval am I chasing? Whose rejection am I most afraid of?

The people you admire, spend time with, and allow to shape your thinking are the people you will become like. Scripture says it simply: *"Walk with the wise and become wise, for a companion of fools suffers harm."* — Proverbs 13:20

If their voices are louder than God's, it's time to make a change. Courage begins by tuning your ear back to Him.

2. Practice Daily Resistance

Conformity happens by default. Transformation happens by decision.

Each morning, surrender your heart again: *"Lord, today I choose You. Your approval over theirs. Your truth over their expectations."*

It might feel small at first — refusing gossip, turning away from compromise, quietly holding your ground — but those small stands become the training ground for stronger convictions. Every small "yes" to God builds courage for the bigger tests ahead.

3. Take One Brave Stand This Week

Don't wait for the perfect moment. Find one place where you've been shrinking back — in a relationship, at work, online — and choose a single step of courage. Speak truth with love. Set a boundary. Share your faith.

Not to prove a point, but to stay true to the One you follow. One stand today becomes the seed of a braver tomorrow.

Don't Get Trapped in the Bait Ball

When you follow the crowd, you may feel hidden. You may feel safe. You may feel accepted — for a while. But like the bait ball in the ocean, every pass of the world's approval takes something from you. Each compromise chips away at your courage and identity.

Little by little, you shrink. You lose your voice. You lose the unique purpose God placed inside you.

But you don't have to stay there. God has called you to more. He has called you to life outside the swirl of fear and compromise. He has called you to follow His cloud — to walk boldly in His presence, even when it feels like you're walking alone.

And when you step out, you will discover this: you are never truly alone. The same Spirit that filled the first disciples with courage fills you now. The same God who split seas and silenced crowds goes before you still. The same Christ who stood alone before Pilate now stands with you.

Choosing the cloud over the crowd won't always be easy. But it will always lead to life — real life. The kind that no cultural wave and no passing opinion can devour.

So, take heart. Start small. Stand firm.

And remember:

better to follow the cloud with courage than to disappear in the swirl of the crowd.

CLOUD MARKER

Don't trade God's presence for people's approval.

Prayer Prompt

Lord, when the pull to blend in feels strong, anchor me again in who I am because of You.

Give me the courage to stand for truth when silence feels safer.

Strip away my need for applause and train my heart to seek Your presence instead.

Form conviction in me where compromise once lived.

Teach me to love people deeply without surrendering truth.

Let my life reflect Your faithfulness—and remind me that I never stand alone.

In Jesus' name, amen.

Reflection Questions

1. When have you felt the strongest pressure to blend in rather than stand out?
2. What "golden calf" or compromise have you been tempted to build in order to keep approval or avoid conflict?
3. Whose opinion feels hardest for you to release right now—and why?
4. Where is God calling you to take one visible step of courage this season?
5. What would it look like to choose courage over silence this week?

Live It Out

Peer pressure doesn't just influence behavior—it reshapes thinking.

That's why Scripture calls you to be **transformed by the renewing of your mind** (Romans 12:2).

This week don't just resist the crowd. **Retrain your thoughts.**

Name the Crowd

Identify one place where approval competes with conviction—a group, environment, or relationship where blending in feels easier than standing firm.

Renew Your Mind

Choose one verse of truth that directly confronts that pressure
(Romans 12:2; Psalm 1:1; Proverbs 13:20).
Write it. Memorize it. Let it govern your response.

Take One Brave Step

Choose one small but faithful action that declares:
I follow the cloud—not the crowd.
Speak when you would stay silent.
Set a boundary.
Change your tone.
Step out in obedience.
Not to be loud—but to be loyal.
Pray. Then act—even if no one else does.
Because transformation never happens by default.
It happens by decision.
And every obedient step builds courage for the next.

CHAPTER 6

FLYING IN FORMATION

Why You Can't Follow the Cloud Alone

*"And let us consider how we may spur one another on toward
love and good deeds, not giving up meeting together, as some are
in the habit of doing, but encouraging one another—and all the
more as you see the Day approaching."*

— HEBREWS 10:24–25

You weren't made to walk alone — God's presence is meant to
be pursued in community.

From the Bait Ball to the V-Formation

In the last chapter, we looked at the bait ball — that frantic swirl of fish
driven by fear and instinct, each one just trying not to be caught. It's
what happens when the crowd takes over: survival replaces direction, fear
replaces discernment, and everyone gets stuck in reactive motion.

No purpose. No leadership. No way out.

But there's another picture in nature — not of panic, but partnership. Look up on a crisp fall morning, and you may see it: geese flying in a perfect V-formation, gliding with quiet power toward a shared destination.

Scientists tell us they fly this way for a reason. The lead bird breaks the headwind, creating uplift for the others. Each one benefits from the one ahead, extending their range by over 70% compared to flying solo. When the leader tires, it drops back, and another takes the front. No ego. No applause. Just rhythm, trust, and lift.

And that honking from below? It's encouragement:

Keep going. We're with you. Don't quit.

It's not just efficient — it's beautiful. And it's biblical.

While the world swirls in bait-ball confusion, chasing trends, shouting opinions, collapsing under pressure, the church is called to move like the geese: lifted by grace, aligned by love, led by the presence of God.

From the beginning, God called a people, not just a person. He rescued a nation, not just Moses. He formed a community before He gave a command.

The more we try to follow Him alone, the more we drift.

Here's the truth:

The crowd will trap you.

The right community will carry you.

The crowd isolates in fear.

A cloud-guided community empowers you to go farther than you ever could alone.

God Never Meant for His People to Fly Alone

From Genesis to Revelation, God has constantly been forming a people, not just gathering isolated individuals. His presence never hovered over lone wanderers; He dwelled among a community on the move.

When He led Israel out of Egypt, He didn't hand Moses a map and say, "Meet Me at the mountain."

He gave them a cloud by day and fire by night — a visible sign of His presence for the whole nation.

They moved together.

Camped together.

Waited together.

Shoulder to shoulder, tribe by tribe, they followed. Even their physical layout reflected this design: every tribe pitched its tents facing the Tent of Meeting, with God's presence at the center.

God wasn't simply guiding individuals. He was forming a community that revolved around His presence.

Fast forward to the New Testament, and the blueprint is the same. When Jesus calls people to follow Him, He doesn't send them off on solo retreats. He invites them into a kingdom, a body, a church — a Spirit-filled, interdependent family.

Even His first disciples were called in pairs. And His final prayer before the cross wasn't for personal success — it was for unity:

"That all of them may be one, Father, just as you are in me and I am in you." — John 17:21

Then came Pentecost. The very first expression of the church after Jesus ascended wasn't a private devotional or an individual conversion story. It's no accident that the same Spirit who once filled the Tabernacle now fills the church.

This wasn't a spiritual flash mob.

It was the beginning of something deeply rooted, intentionally formed, and Spirit-empowered.

The message is unmistakable: belonging and doing life together in community matters.

If you have been freed from the chains that once bound you, you were placed into a people — not just liberated from sin.

So when we treat church as optional, community as inconvenient, and belonging as negotiable, we're not just resisting organized religion… we're resisting God's design.

The world might tell you faith is personal.

Jesus shows us that faith is also relational.

And the cloud?

It still moves.

But it doesn't move with spiritual freelancers.

It moves with His people — the church.

Jesus Builds a People, Not Just Converts
(Matthew 16:18)

When Jesus gathered His disciples in Caesarea Philippi — a place filled with altars to pagan gods and political powers — He asked the question that would shape eternity:

"Who do you say I am?" — Matthew 16:15

Peter responded: *"You are the Messiah, the Son of the living God."*
And Jesus didn't say, *"Great answer — now go live a private spiritual life."*
He said:

"On this rock I will build my church, and the gates of Hades will not overcome it." (v. 18)

Let that sink in:

The very first time Jesus mentions His vision for the future, He says, ***"I will build my church."***

The word Jesus used for church — ekklesia — wasn't religious. It referred to an assembly: a gathered group of citizens called out to move and govern together. Jesus could've said "temple" or "synagogue." But He chose ekklesia— not a building but a body of people. And He made it clear: "I will build my church." It's His design, His mission, His movement — and nothing, not even the gates of Hades, will stop it.

And notice: He doesn't say, *"You will build the church."*

He says, *"I will."*

It's His project. His design. His house.

That means when we minimize church, avoid it, or try to follow Jesus without it…

We're rejecting the very thing He came to build.

If you claim to love Jesus but reject His church, you're saying "yes" to the Groom but "no" to the Bride.

It's tempting in today's culture to say, *"I'm spiritual but not religious,"* or *"I love Jesus, but I'm done with church."*

But Jesus never gave that option.

And the promise is clear:

When we gather around that confession — 'You are the Messiah, the Son of the living God' — Jesus Himself promises to build His church among us.

The church is not an afterthought — a last-minute, put-together plan. It was in the mind of God from the very beginning. Paul put it this way:

"His intent was that now, through the church, the manifold wisdom of God should be made known to the rulers and authorities in the heavenly realms, according to his eternal purpose that he accomplished in Christ Jesus our Lord." — Ephesians 3:10–11

Before the first sunrise, before the first breath of Adam, the church was already part of God's eternal purpose. Jesus is building something unshakable — and He's been planning it since before the foundation of the world.

So if you're longing for purpose, strength, and spiritual growth, you don't need to go off and start something new. You need to root yourself in what Jesus is already building.

The question is no longer, *"Who do you say Jesus is?"*

It's also, "Are you willing to follow Him into community — the way He designed it?"

The Cloud Descends Again at Pentecost
(Acts 2)

If Jesus promised to build His church, Pentecost was the grand opening.

In Acts 2, the disciples were together in one place — united in prayer. Then it happened:

A sound like a violent wind filled the house, and tongues of fire rested on each of them (Acts 2:2–3).

Wind. Fire. Presence.

The same God who descended at Sinai, who filled the Tabernacle, who led His people through the wilderness — now comes not to dwell in a tent, but in His people.

And it doesn't fall on one superstar disciple.

It falls on all of them — not as reward, but as fulfillment of God's promise to pour out His Spirit on all flesh.

Peter connects the dots: Jesus is Lord and Messiah. The crowd is cut to the heart. His answer isn't, "Go pray alone," but:

"Repent and be baptized, every one of you… and you will receive the gift of the Holy Spirit." (Acts 2:38).

What follows is the clearest picture of following the cloud:

"They devoted themselves to the apostles' teaching and to fellowship, to the breaking of bread and to prayer… All the believers were together… And the Lord added to their number daily" (Acts 2:42–47).

This is what the Spirit produces — not just power, but community:

- Shared life
- Mutual devotion
- Spirit-led belonging

The God who once moved above His people in a cloud now moves within them, binding them into a new kind of family. The same wind that fills your lungs pushes you into community.

The Presence descended again.

Not on a mountain.

Not in a temple.

But in us.

The Cloud Crosses Every Line

Pentecost gathered Jews, but it was anything but monocultural. Luke says there were *"God-fearing Jews from every nation under heaven"* (Acts 2:5). They came from Africa, Arabia, Persia, Rome, and Asia — speaking different languages, carrying different customs and tensions.

Different looks. Different voices. Different minds.

And yet, the Spirit fell on all of them — not to erase their distinctions, but to unite them in something deeper than culture. The cloud doesn't gather sameness; it gathers surrender.

From the beginning, the church was meant to reflect unity deeper than bloodline or background — a unity rooted in God's presence. That same Spirit is still forming a church today — one that reflects heaven's diversity, not culture's division.

But the story didn't stop at Pentecost. One wall still stood: Gentiles. In Acts 10, the Spirit falls on Cornelius, a Roman centurion and outsider. Peter, once convinced salvation was for Israel alone, watches the same Spirit descend on Gentiles and admits:

"God does not show favoritism but accepts from every nation the one who fears Him and does what is right" (Acts 10:34–35).

Later: *"They have received the Holy Spirit just as we have. So who am I to stand in God's way?"*

This was no small shift — it collapsed a centuries-old wall. From Babel to Sinai to Pentecost to Cornelius, the cloud was always moving toward this: one people, made not by race, tribe, or law, but by the Spirit of the Living God.

The world says divide.

The Spirit says belong.

The cloud crosses every line.

So when we reduce church to a social club, a style preference, or a safe echo chamber of people who look, vote, or think like us — we've missed the point.

If the Spirit tears down walls, who are we to rebuild them?

Following the cloud means following with others — showing up, breaking bread, praying together, and devoting yourself not just to God, but to God's people.

The Church Is the Cloud's Movement Today

We say we want to be Spirit-led — to know God's will, feel His presence, and follow His lead. But the Spirit doesn't just guide individuals; He guides a people. Discernment was never meant to happen in isolation.

The church isn't a weekly event or a spiritual pit stop. It's the living body of Christ — the continuation of God's presence on earth. The cloud that once hovered over the Tabernacle and descended in fire at Pentecost now moves through His people.

When we treat church like a podcast to watch or a product to consume, we miss the design. Scripture assumes something deeper: that every Christian is using their gifts to build up the body. *"Each of you should use whatever gift you have received to serve others, as faithful stewards of God's grace in its various forms."* — 1 Peter 4:10

You belong to one another. You walk under the care of godly leaders who shepherd and teach. And you live out the "one another" commands — love, forgive, encourage, bear with, and instruct. None of these makes sense in isolation. They only come alive in committed fellowship.

You can't obey Jesus while ignoring His people.

You can't follow Christ while walking away from His body.

You weren't made to drift. You were made to belong.

Belonging means covenant, not convenience. This is why Hebrews reminds us: *"Let us not give up meeting together, as some are in the habit of doing, but encourage one another — and all the more as you see the Day approaching."* — Hebrews 10:25

As the world grows more isolated, skeptical, and spiritually numb, the church becomes more essential — not less. Not just for your growth, but for your survival.

The crowd is still swirling — loud, reactive, collapsing in panic.

But the formation flight of faith is still moving forward — a people lifted by presence, not fear.

The question is: Which one are you in?

1. Crowds That Pull You Away

Environments shaped by conformity, not conviction. They resist truth, downplay devotion, and eventually drift you out of alignment with God's presence.

> *"Do not be yoked together with unbelievers. For what do righteousness and wickedness have in common? Or what fellowship can light have with darkness?"* — 2 Corinthians 6:14

Like Israel at Sinai, crowds trade waiting on God for worshiping something else. They promise speed and excitement but leave you emptier than before.

2. Circles That Keep You Still

Safe but stagnant. You may share history or hobbies, but not hunger. They don't sharpen you or call you deeper. And over time, you'll match their lukewarm faith.

> *"As iron sharpens iron, so one person sharpens another."*
> — Proverbs 27:17

3. Communities That Call You Higher

These keep your eyes on the cloud. They pray when you're weary, speak truth when you want to run, and lift you when you're weak (Exodus 17:12). They don't compete but complete; they don't just stay for the mountaintop but walk with you through the valley.

This is what Jesus built with His disciples, what the early church embodied — and what's still possible today.

The Power of a Cloud-Chasing Community

This isn't just theory — I've lived it. For more than two decades, I've flown in formation with a circle of servant leaders who are far more than co-laborers — they are my brothers: Carlos Scott, Abou Djaouga, Raynold Mensah, Wayne Billups, Darryl Grady, Willis Thomas, and Tony Steward — my brother-in-law. And my brother from the same mother, Larry Reed Jr.

Along with their wives, they've been pillars in my life. And one of them shares my home: Charon, my wife, my partner in ministry and in life for over thirty-five years.

With the exception of my brother Larry, who serves in the ministry in Massachusetts, we don't just serve together in our local church — we fight for each other's faith. We've prayed through heartbreak, spoken life into doubt, and stood shoulder-to-shoulder when storms have hit. We've walked through dry seasons, family crises, ministry pressures, and personal pain — not as scattered believers scrambling to survive, but as a formation that refuses to leave anyone behind.

Our unity isn't built on personality or convenience. It's built on a shared hunger to follow the cloud — wherever it leads. And they have been my lifeline in more ways than I can count.

Looking back, every major spiritual breakthrough in my life traces back to one common denominator:

I wasn't walking alone.

I've been in crowds that distracted me.

I've stayed in circles that kept me still.

But the defining moments — the turning points of growth, conviction, and calling — always came when I was surrounded by people who refused to let me fly solo.

I remember seasons when my faith felt dry and routine. When it was a task to read the word, share my faith, and give to others. There were times when I didn't want to go to church, when I wasn't fulfilled. Without even knowing it, I was drifting.

And in His mercy, God always placed people in my life who wouldn't let me stay there. They didn't coddle me — they called me higher. They didn't trail behind — they flew beside.

That's what a cloud-chasing community does.

You don't need a perfect church.

You need people who hunger for God's presence and won't settle for anything less.

It's not just about hearing from God — it's about walking with those who won't let you stop.

So don't get caught in the swirl of the bait ball.

Find your formation.

Follow the cloud.

And fly farther than you ever could alone.

Because when you lock wings with the right people, you discover what the geese already know: the journey is longer, the lift is stronger, and together, you'll make it home.

And don't just join the formation — be the reason it flies farther.

CLOUD MARKER

**You weren't made to fly solo — find your formation
and follow the cloud together.**

Prayer Prompt

Lord, I'm tired of flying alone.

I've tried to carry the weight myself, and I've felt the drift that comes when I do.

But You never designed the journey to be solitary.

Help me find my formation.

Surround me with cloud-chasers who strengthen me, challenge me, and keep me aligned with Your movement.

And shape me into someone who lifts others, not just someone who needs lifting.

Teach me to fly in step with Your Spirit and in rhythm with Your people. In Jesus' name, amen.

Reflection Questions

1. Who is currently shaping your spiritual formation—and where are they helping you fly stronger or drift weaker?
2. Have you ever stepped away from community because of pain, disappointment, or pride? What would it look like to return wisely, not guardedly?
3. Where are you trying to lead on your own when God may be calling you to receive support instead?
4. Who do you need to lift right now—and who do you need to allow to lift you?

Live It Out

This week, take one intentional step back into formation.

- Reach out to someone you trust and ask, *"Can we pray together this week?"*
- Join—or rejoin—a small group, Bible study, or church gathering, even if it feels uncomfortable at first.
- Notice someone who is flying tired and choose to walk—or fly—beside them.
- Show up not just to attend, but to connect, contribute, and be known.

Don't drift.

Don't fly solo.

Find your formation—and help someone else find theirs.

CHAPTER 7

FOLLOWING THE CLOUD THROUGH PEOPLE AND PLACES

How God's Presence Shapes Us Through Community

Therefore, encourage one another and build each other up,
just as in fact you are doing."
— 1 THESSALONIANS 5:11

God builds His people through His people

THIS CHAPTER IS different—and that's on purpose.

We've been talking about following the cloud—not alone, but in formation. In the last chapter, we explored how God uses relationships to steady us, shape us, and help us soar.

But what does that actually look like in real life?

What happens when the cloud moves through people—not just to help you belong, but to build you? What does it mean to be stretched, challenged, and changed by the communities God places in your path?

This chapter explores a central theme in my life story—my testimony about community. It's a walk through the places and people who carried the cloud for me—mentors, churches, and spiritual voices God used to form my faith.

Every believer's story has markers. These are mine—and I share them in the hope that you'll recognize your own.

Although this chapter is shaped by my story, my hope is that it ultimately helps you see yours. As you read, I invite you to reflect on the ways God has been nudging, pulling, and guiding you—often through the people He's placed in your life.

Along the way, consider these questions:

- How has God moved in your life? Did anyone carry the cloud for you, pointing you to Christ and a deeper relationship with God?
- Who believed in you, challenged you, or walked beside you while you were still growing—or struggling?
- If you haven't in the past—or aren't currently—walking with a cloud-chasing community, what might it look like to seek one now?

Because that's how God works. He forms us—and stretches us—through people, through a love that goes beyond our preferences, our past, and our expectations.

Northeast Church of Christ — 13th and Hopkins Street, Milwaukee, WI

Where My Faith Journey Began

Milwaukee—a foundation of faith that would shape every step to come.

Every faith story begins somewhere.

Mine began in a small brick building on the north side of Milwaukee, on the corner of 13th and Hopkins Street.

It was a congregation of ordinary people with extraordinary convictions.

But its beginning wasn't easy. The church was born out of conflict that demanded courage. In the early 1960s, questioning church leadership could get you pushed out.

My grandmother, Odessa Avery—who we affectionately called Gang-Gan—was a strong woman of faith. She knew the Bible, loved to teach, and wasn't afraid to stand for what was right.

She had been studying Scripture with a young man in the congregation who was eager to grow. He asked her to help him understand the Bible more accurately—and she did. But the preacher at the time objected. The studies were happening without his permission, and he saw that as rebellion.

During a Sunday service, he announced from the pulpit that the young man was being disfellowshipped for refusing to stop the studies. My grandmother spoke up—not out of disrespect, but because what was happening was wrong.

The preacher turned to her and said,

"If you say another word, Odessa, I'll write your name down and withdraw from you too."

She spoke again.

And he did.

My grandfather, Quiller Harris, stood with her and was also disfellowshipped. In that moment, they were pushed out of their church.

But that moment became the beginning of something new.

In February 1963, seven believers—including my grandparents—began meeting on their own. Their first services were held in a rented upstairs room next to a bar on Clarke Street. Later, they moved to 13th and Hopkins Street. That's how the Northeast Church of Christ was born.

No money. No staff. Just conviction—and a desire to follow God.

My grandfather became the minister. He wasn't flashy, but he loved the Bible and preached it faithfully. I still remember him saying, *"Just show me in the Script."*

And when someone asked a question, he'd reply,

"What does the Script say?"

That congregation laid the foundation for my faith.

It's where I first heard the gospel.

Where I saw courage lived out.

Where I learned that real faith doesn't retreat when things get uncomfortable.

I was baptized there as a young teenager, coming forward with my brother and sister during the invitation song—probably *Just As I Am*. That moment confirmed what had already been forming in my heart: I was claiming for myself the faith I had received.

Northeast wasn't just the first church I attended.

It was where I learned to follow the cloud, not the crowd.

And from that little brick building on 13th and Hopkins, the cloud would rise again—leading to new places, new seasons, and new people who would carry God's presence in ways I never could have imagined.

Second Missionary Baptist Church — Centralia, IL
The Congregation That Birthed My Wife's Faith

God doesn't shape us only through our own roots—He also shapes us through the faith of those we will one day walk beside. For me, that meant the church that formed my wife.

Founded in 1869 by formerly enslaved believers and freedom-seekers, Second Missionary Baptist has endured fires, cultural upheaval, and generations of change. Yet one conviction—their congregational motto—has never wavered: **Christ first. Ourselves second.**

This is the soil that formed Charon—where Scripture took root, faith matured, and compassion for God's people was cultivated. I see that heritage in her wisdom, her service, and her steady strength.

Second Baptist has also been a quiet anchor for our family. In one of my darkest valleys, marked by illness and loss, they prayed for me from hundreds of miles away—their intercession wrapping around me like armor.

I'm especially grateful for my in-laws, whose faith has quietly steadied both our family and this congregation for decades. My father-in-law, Deacon Rufus Hill, embodies faithful, unseen service. And my mother-in-law's life of sacrificial love for family carries the same steady heartbeat: **serving others matters.**

From this enduring lighthouse in Centralia, the cloud rose again—guiding Charon to a small college town where our paths would finally meet.

Macomb Church of Christ — Macomb, IL
My College Refuge and Home Away from Home

This is where I learned that spiritual family can transcend culture—and where calling can be born in the quiet corners of a college town.

Macomb, Illinois, was nothing like Milwaukee.

It was smaller. Quieter. And as a young African American student-athlete arriving at Western Illinois University, it felt worlds away from everything I knew.

I didn't just need structure.

I needed belonging.

I needed sanctuary.

That's what the Macomb Church of Christ became for me—not just a place to attend, but a home where I was known and welcomed.

In a town where I could have been reduced to my jersey or my skin color, this church reminded me of something greater: I was a child of God. A brother. A friend. A son.

Their hospitality wasn't accidental; it was intentional. They didn't try to shape me into a mold. They made room for my presence, my questions, my culture, and my growth.

This small congregation, with roots stretching back to 1845, quietly lived out a powerful truth:

True Christian community isn't about looking alike—it's about looking to Christ together.

Within that community were shepherds—faithful, prayerful leaders who held me steady during one of the most formative seasons of my life. I am forever grateful for

Numa and Ruth Crowder,

Ray and June Martin,

Jack and Violet Beard,

Larry and Ann Morley,

and John and Alice Sullivan.

They fed me.

They prayed for me.

They taught me.

They loved me.

In their homes, I found peace.

In their lives, I saw shepherding modeled—not with titles, but with tenderness.

It wasn't in a classroom or a conference, but in the living rooms of faithful saints, that God planted a vision for ministry in my heart. They didn't push me toward leadership. They loved me—and that love did the shaping.

The Macomb Church of Christ formed me not because it was big or impressive, but because it was faithful.

Through them, I learned again that the cloud doesn't only move through circumstances—it moves through people who carry God's presence into your life. And when the season of shelter has done its work, the cloud begins to rise.

The God who comforts also calls.

When the cloud lifted from Macomb, it wasn't to send me wandering—it was to lead me home.

If Macomb was my refuge, Lakeview would become my refining furnace.

Lakeview Church of Christ — Milwaukee, WI
The Community That Called Me Higher

From refuge to refining — that's what Lakeview became for me. A place where God wasn't just sheltering me but stripping me down to rebuild my heart around lordship.

I didn't arrive at Lakeview broken.

I arrived ready to serve.

Fresh out of college. Back in my hometown. Energized. Gifted. Eager.

But God had a different agenda.

He wasn't recruiting talent — He was after the heart.

If you've ever thought God wanted skills more than surrender, you know how disorienting it feels when He points past the gifts and goes straight for the core of who you are.

Lakeview was barely a year old — a bold, young church plant in the heart of Milwaukee. What it lacked in size or polish, it made up for in spiritual fire.

This wasn't just a congregation — it was a furnace.

And I was about to be refined.

The lead minister, Eric Mansfield, didn't preach for applause. He preached for repentance.

With Spirit-filled boldness and fatherly love, he saw through the surface — past the religious résumé and the good intentions — and named the duplicity I hadn't dared to admit.

His words didn't shame — they awakened.

For the first time, it became clear: Jesus wasn't asking to be added to a life already in motion.

He was demanding all of it.

At Lakeview, Lordship came into focus.

It wasn't church attendance.

It wasn't moral effort.

It wasn't using gifts for God while keeping certain rooms of the heart locked.

It was surrender.

Total. Undivided. Undiluted.

The obvious sins were confessed.

The rationalized ones were dragged into the light.

Even the pride I hadn't seen — the kind that warps how you see others and yourself — had to go. God pulled back the curtain, and the truth was undeniable.

When the moment came, I chose to hit the restart button on my walk—and I was baptized. Not because I doubted God's grace, but to draw a line. Not to erase the story, but to re-center it under the rightful King.

The belief had always been there—even the commitment. Now, there was trust — trust in Jesus as the risen Savior and, especially, as the reigning Lord.

There's been no looking back.

Lakeview became the turning point — shaping character, teaching that real love doesn't flatter but tells the truth, walks with you through the mess, anchors you in grace, and refuses to let you settle for a half-lived faith.

It was the fire that didn't just refine — it set a life ablaze.

From the heat of that furnace, the cloud rose again — this time toward a city that would stretch vision, deepen conviction, and teach how to plant seeds of the gospel in entirely new soil.

Detroit Church of Christ — Detroit, MI
The Church Plant That Strengthened Our Mission.

God doesn't refine us to keep us in place. The cloud rose again—this time not for shelter, but for mission.

After several formative years in Milwaukee, Charon—then my girlfriend—and I were invited into a bold church-planting mission in Detroit. There was no hesitation. The answer was yes. Not yes to a city, but yes to a calling larger than us.

Our mission was both simple and staggering: build campus ministries from the ground up—the same kind that once transformed our lives, now entrusted to us to pass on.

Alongside faithful dreamers—Rodney and Jennifer Fuller, Micky Tan, Shannon Wright, and Rick and Diana Stafford—we began planting seeds at Eastern Michigan University, the University of Michigan, and eventually Wayne State.

And God moved.

Bible discussions started. Students gathered. Hearts opened. Lives changed.

Under the leadership of Kevin and Traecena Holland—visionaries marked by joy, conviction, and deep belief in people—the ministries multiplied. But the growth went deeper than numbers. Unity thickened. Faith expanded. The Spirit's momentum was unmistakable.

About a year in, Charon and I were asked to leave our jobs and step into full-time ministry. It was a defining crossroads—and once again, the answer was yes.

That season became a masterclass in leadership, learned in living rooms and late-night prayers. I discovered that vision fuels mission, trust grows best in hard soil, and even one transformed soul is worth everything.

Detroit was gritty. Demanding. Beautiful.

It strengthened our faith and softened our hearts.

It taught us that the gospel doesn't avoid hard places—it flourishes there.

Looking back, I see it clearly now: God wasn't only planting a church in Detroit. He was planting something in us—a deeper conviction, a broader vision, and a readiness for what was to come.

From the grit and glory of Detroit, the cloud rose once more—this time toward Chicago, where that calling would be tested, refined, and shaped for the seasons ahead.

Oak Park / Chicago Church of Christ — Chicago, IL
The Church That Refined My Calling

From Detroit, God led us into a wider field—a place where vision would be tested and calling refined.

Long before I arrived, Chicagoland had already stirred something in me. As a college student, hearing Marty Fuqua preach with bold conviction and a heart for Chicago ignited a vision that quietly shaped my early faith.

Years later, while we were on our mission in Detroit, the invitation to serve in Chicago came. Charon and I moved to Oak Park with an infant son and open hearts. We were embraced by leaders who became family—especially Ron and Lavonia Drabot. Fresh from Johannesburg, they poured wisdom, love, and steady guidance into our lives at just the right time.

Serving across the west side, south side, and downtown, my calling wasn't merely affirmed—it was sharpened. We were given room to lead, to stumble, to learn, and to grow.

As the Chicago Church of Christ expanded, "Operation Saturation" revealed both the passion and the pressure of a movement growing faster than it could breathe. In that season, Charon and I were appointed ministry leaders—not as a title to carry, but as a trust God had been preparing us to steward.

Chicago became a classroom. Vision stretched. Endurance deepened. Leadership was forged. Grace was learned through surrender. The lessons from Oak Park, the Southside, and downtown still shape how we serve today.

And then the cloud rose again—to California, Ohio, and eventually the nation's capital.

Chicago didn't just refine my ministry.

It refined my heart for what was coming ahead.

DC Regional Christian Church — Hillcrest Heights, MD
Where We Serve, Grow, and Continue to Be Shaped

The cloud doesn't only lead through growth. Sometimes it leads through fire—through pruning and disappointment—to prepare us for what's next.

After Chicago, as our fellowship circles entered a season of strain, our dependence on God deepened. What followed was a whirlwind—California, Ohio, then the East Coast—guided not by a roadmap, but by a single burden: follow wherever God leads, even when nothing feels certain.

Each stop stretched us. New assignments. Lean finances. Spiritual pressure that settled in like fog. Some days felt like walking with no horizon, holding only the quiet assurance that God was still out front.

But God wasn't just moving us. He was reshaping us.

We began to see how a system chasing numbers can drift from spiritual health—how Christ can be overshadowed and the Spirit muted. The disillusionment was real, but so was God's steady voice: *Don't cling to what's shaking. Keep following Me.*

So we did.

Every stop became both proving ground and gift. Hearts were refined—not in comfort, but in fire. Like Israel at the Red Sea, hemmed in on every side, we learned to move forward even when the way wasn't clear.

God was pruning.

God was preparing.

And the cloud kept leading.

A New Beginning in the DMV

In 2003, DC Regional Christian Church was born—not to preserve a system, but to pursue a Spirit-led vision. Alongside lifelong friends Carlos and Cassandra Scott and a team of servant-hearted leaders, we stepped into a new chapter: Christ-centered, Spirit-empowered, and rooted in God's Word.

Soon after, Abou and Contina Djaouga returned from mission work in Fiji to join us, bringing global vision and renewed strength. The team was formed. The mission was clear.

From the beginning, our aim wasn't to replicate the past, but to reimagine what church could be—anchored in Scripture, alive with the Spirit, and united around Christ. We longed for the unity Jesus prayed for—a unity that rises above traditions and man-made boundaries.

So we chose not to burn bridges, but to build them. To focus on what matters most:

Are we following Jesus?

Surrendered to the Spirit?

Rooted in the Word?

Living the Great Commandment and the Great Commission?

"The Lord knows those who are his." — 2 Timothy 2:19

As we relaunched, *Follow the Cloud, Not the Crowd* became our guiding conviction—not a slogan, but a posture. A commitment to pursue God's presence over popularity and to follow wherever He leads.

That conviction still leads us.

Twenty years later, DC Regional isn't just a church we serve—it's a family we love. It's where God continues to stretch us, shape us, and send us.

We haven't arrived—and we don't intend to.

We're still learning.

Still growing.

Still trusting.

Still following the cloud.

When the Cloud Moves Beyond the Camp

"Now Moses used to take a tent and pitch it outside the camp..."
— Exodus 33:7

"Let us, then, go to him outside the camp..." — Hebrews 13:13

Sometimes following the cloud means stepping beyond the camp—beyond comfort, tradition, and the expectations of the crowd. Not to abandon your people, but to seek the God who leads you further.

Moses did it in the wilderness.

Jesus did it through the cross.

And now we are called to do the same.

This isn't about leaving your spiritual roots; it's about choosing Jesus over the approval of your circle. Often, the places others overlook are where His voice speaks most clearly.

Not everyone understood the direction God was leading us—and yes, it hurt. Heritage matters. But the cloud doesn't always move within familiar lanes. God was calling us to grow beyond tribal expectations.

So we followed the Spirit.

We stayed connected through relationships while remaining free from distant control—anchored in truth, united in love, and led by the same cloud that guides all who seek Him. When God stretches vision, it unsettles those who prefer things as they were.

So we chose obedience.

That meant drinking from wells we didn't dig, sitting at tables we didn't build, and hearing God speak through unexpected voices. Then came a freeing realization:

The Spirit of God is not confined to tribes or camps.

He moves wherever hearts are surrendered.

He speaks through anyone submitted to His Word.

If we stay humble, we will find Him in places we once assumed we wouldn't.

Learning Beyond Our Traditions

From the beginning, we knew we couldn't do this alone. If the Church is truly a body, no single part carries all the wisdom. So we chose to learn—and to listen.

In 2006, our leadership team attended the Purpose-Driven Church Conference, seeking insight beyond the familiar. What stood out wasn't size, but humility. Narrow lanes opened into a wide field of God's grace. I saw that God was doing far more, in far more places, than the world I had grown up inside.

The distinction became clear: some matters are major, others are not—but Jesus must remain the center. Faithfulness means following the cloud wherever He leads.

So we kept learning—through friendships, conversations, and shared mission across traditions. What mattered wasn't labels, but Jesus.

And even now, we're still listening.

Still willing to learn.

Still following wherever the cloud leads—

because in every season, God has carried His presence into our lives through His people.

Your Story Is Being Shaped, Too

These are my markers. Yours may look different — and that's the point. The same God who shaped me through people and places is shaping you too.

Every place in this chapter is more than geography — it's testimony.

Every circumstance, every church, every relationship, every joy and hardship wasn't just a season — it was a shaping space. A sacred stop on a journey God Himself was leading.

But this isn't just my story.

It's an invitation to reflect on yours.

Maybe you've found a Christ-centered community that calls you higher.

Maybe you're still searching — or still healing.

Maybe the church that once helped you can't hold who you're becoming.

Wherever you are, hear this:

Across rural and urban churches, Black and White congregations, Baptist roots and Restoration branches, I've seen God's Spirit move through His people and transform lives.

God forms us through people — not perfect ones, but faithful ones.

People who sharpen us, stretch us, and walk beside us.

People who remind us who we are when we forget.

I often think of my grandmother, Gang-Gan — standing in that little Milwaukee church with nothing but conviction and courage. She had no idea her decision that day would ripple into generations. She only knew she had to be faithful.

That's how God works.

Faithfulness in one person, in one moment, can shape a family line, a church, even a future.

Maybe the people who shaped you never knew the impact they had. Maybe they still don't. But God knew — and He used them to carry His presence into your life.

So pause and consider:

Who helped you become more like Christ?

What communities built your faith — and which ones pulled you away?

Is God inviting you to re-engage, forgive, or help build something new?

And what kind of community are *you* shaping for someone else?

Every step of faith is shaped by the people and places God weaves into our journey. We're called to build one another up (1 Thessalonians 5:11) — to reflect Christ not just with our lives, but with our love.

So, as you look back, don't just remember — recognize.

See the cloud markers: the mentors, friends, churches, and moments that helped you follow God's presence.

See how He carried His presence into your life through people and places you never expected.

And then — look forward.

Someone is walking behind you.

Someone is searching for a community to remind them who they are in Christ… and who they're becoming.

Let's be those people.

Let's be that kind of church.

Let's follow the cloud through people and places — with the same courage my grandmother showed that day — and help others do the same. Together.

CLOUD MARKER

The people you walk with shape who you become — choose companions who help you follow the cloud.

Prayer Prompt

Lord, thank You for the people and communities that shaped my faith.

Open my eyes to those walking beside me now — those who strengthen me and those who need encouragement.

Form me within a community that reflects Your presence, speaks truth with love, and walks in step with You.

Use my life to build others up as You have built me.

In Jesus' name, amen.

Reflection Questions

1. What kind of Christ-centered community do you long for, and what has kept you from pursuing it?

2. Who in your life reflects a faith that draws you closer to Christ — and how might God be using them to guide your next step?

3. How are you shaping the culture of your community right now — through your words, presence, and consistency?

4. What spiritual legacy are you building through the people you walk with?

Live It Out

This week:

- Reach out to someone who has shaped your faith and thank them.
- Ask God to reveal one person you can intentionally encourage or walk alongside.
- Show up as the kind of community you once prayed for.

Walk wisely.

The cloud often leads through people.

CHAPTER 8

THE POWER OF QUIET

When God Speaks Softly, and Trust Learns to Listen

*"But when you pray, go into your room, close the door, and pray
to your Father, who is unseen. Then your Father, who sees
what is done in secret, will reward you."*

— MATTHEW 6:6

When you enter the quiet, God enters with His presence.

When Every Other Voice Fades

"My sheep listen to my voice; I know them, and they follow me."
— John 10:27

The room can be full of voices. Friends encouraging. Mentors advising.
Pastors preaching. Podcasts filling the air. And yet — silence inside.

But no matter how many voices fill the air, only one can lead you
forward.

I've walked with some of the godliest people — shepherds who guided me, brothers who prayed with me, friends who stood beside me. But here's what I've learned: their support and voices can strengthen you, but they cannot substitute for Him.

No community can replace communion with the Creator.

No sermon can replace the leadership of the Spirit.

No friend.

No mentor.

Not even the best of them.

And, if we're not careful, even good voices become part of the noise. We lean on secondhand wisdom — disciplers, pastors, podcasts, books. All good gifts. But over time, our ears grow attuned to them... and lose the sound of Him.

I've been there. Have you?

We don't mean to replace His voice. But we do. And when we do, intimacy slips away.

Here's what I have come to know: the voices may guide you.

But only the Shepherd can lead you.

He still knows you. He's still speaking.

And His sheep still follow — if they listen.

When God Interrupted My Prayer

"Why are you doing all the talking?"

The question hit me halfway through my prayers on a trail I'd walked for years — Sligo Creek Parkway.

I've worn grooves in that path with prayer: blossoms in spring, blazing leaves in fall, the icy breath of winter mornings. The air smells of damp earth and maple leaves. The creek runs low and steady beside the trail, a sound you can almost pray in rhythm to. For me, it's sacred ground.

For years, my prayers followed the same pattern: begin with the Lord's Prayer, then praise, then thanksgiving, then requests. Asking God to move, to fill, to act. A comfortable routine I could pray in my sleep.

But that day, the routine broke open. Not an audible voice. Not a flash of light. Just a quiet interruption in my spirit — a question I couldn't ignore.

Why are you doing all the talking?

I froze mid-stride. I realized I'd been praying earnestly, but not listening. So I stopped.

For the first time in a long time, I didn't rush to fill the air. I prayed, "Lord, speak to me?" Then I walked slowly. Listening.

The only sounds were my footsteps on the path and the steady murmur of the creek. Sometimes I sat on a bench, still and unhurried. I didn't force anything. I just gave God space.

And He met me there — not in my words, but in the silence.

The Shepherd's Whisper

In the hush of the quiet, His voice is never absent.

The Shepherd of my soul speaks — sometimes with a word I've heard before, sometimes with a whisper that feels brand new. But always with exactly what I need.

He anchors me in love — love that steadies, secures, and holds me when the ground shifts.

He convicts me — pressing on the places where trust must deepen, where pride must yield, where change cannot wait.

He places names on my heart — family, friends, church, neighbors, even strangers — nudges to pray, to check in, to call.

He stills my restless spirit, leading me beside quiet waters until my soul remembers how to breathe again.

And then He does what only He can:

He breathes faith into fear.

He infuses courage where I had none.

He opens my eyes to wisdom I could never see alone.

But this I know above all: whatever His words, however they come, His voice always carries the same call —

"Daryl, follow Me."

The War for Your Attention

Here's the challenge — mine and yours: we can't follow a voice we can't hear. And we can't hear if we don't prioritize time with Him.

Jesus told Martha, *"You are worried and upset about many things, but few things are needed — or indeed only one"* — Luke 10:41–42. That moment wasn't just about her kitchen. It was about us.

We live in a world of *"many things."* They don't just keep us busy — they keep us from hearing the one thing that matters most.

"Can I get some peace and quiet around here!?" We say it when the kids are loud, the phone won't stop buzzing, or the headlines won't stop breaking. But beneath the frustration is a deeper ache: we're starving for stillness in a world that never shuts up.

Our culture is addicted to input — notifications, news, endless noise. Sometimes the "crowd" is literal, pressing in on us like it did on Jesus. But more often it isn't people at all. It's pressure. It's pace. Many things.

From the moment we wake, alarms, texts, reels, and ads fight for our attention. Even in an empty room, our minds hum with noise, shaping us without permission. No wonder we're restless. No wonder we confuse movement for progress and distraction for productivity.

Yet something in us knows: we weren't made for this. We crave something quieter. More grounded. A space where God can be heard again.

I've had to say it out loud: "Enough with the noise."

No more scrolling.

No more chasing what doesn't satisfy.

No more distractions disguised as purpose.

Instead, I fight to treasure what I treasure:

A quiet walk with God.

An open Bible.

A still heart.

I come to understand why monks fled to deserts. St. Anthony once said:

> "He who sits alone and is quiet has escaped from three wars: hearing, speaking, and seeing. Yet there is one thing against which he must continually fight: his own heart."

He was right. The war isn't just around us. The fiercest battle is often within.

The Storm Inside

Let's lean in on this: the noise within us.

Even when the room is silent, our thoughts start shouting:

You should be farther by now.

You're falling behind.

What if you fail?

What will they think?

Regret loops from the past. Fear reaches from the future. The moment we try to pray, we're pulled everywhere but present.

Often it's not that we don't want God — it's that we're afraid of what His voice will uncover when everything else fades. Grief rises. Doubt surfaces. Buried insecurities come knocking. We blame our phones or schedules, but the real distraction storm is inside of us.

Here's the good news: God isn't afraid of your storm. He isn't irritated by anxious thoughts. He doesn't come to shame you. He comes to walk with you.

In the quiet, He restores. He draws you close. And maybe the silence you've been avoiding is the very space where He wants to heal you — where He reminds you who you really are.

And if you've ever wondered how God meets someone in that place — when the inner roar is deafening and the weight feels too heavy — you're not the first. Elijah knew it well. One of God's boldest prophets, he too reached the breaking point, overwhelmed by the noise outside and the storm inside.

And what God whispered to him may be exactly what He's whispering to you.

Lessons from Elijah — How the Whisper Breaks the Inner Roar

Elijah lived in one of Israel's darkest seasons. He stood against kings, called down fire from heaven, and proved the Lord alone is God. Yet right after the triumph on Mount Carmel, he collapsed. One threat from Jezebel sent him running into the wilderness, begging God to take his life.

And how did God respond? Not with rebuke. Not with shame. He gave Elijah rest, bread, and water. Then He led him to Mount Horeb — the mountain of God.

There Elijah braced for the dramatic — wind, earthquake, fire. But God wasn't in any of them. He came in a gentle whisper.

Not in the noise.

Not in the spectacle.

But in the still, small voice.

That whisper pierced Elijah's fear and reminded him: God's presence isn't found in fireworks or crowds, but in the quietest places — even in a cave, even in exhaustion.

And that same God still meets us there.

He kneels where we collapse.

He feeds us when we faint.

He whispers when we weep.

He calls us when we cannot stand.

The God who calls us to courage is the same God who cares for us in weakness.

That's who He was for Elijah.

That's who He is for you — revealed perfectly in Jesus.

God's Voice Is in the Quiet, Not the Chaos

Elijah expected God in the wind, the quake, the fire. Instead, He came in a whisper — a sound so easy to miss unless you're still enough to listen.

We're conditioned to look for Him in the big moments — miracles, breakthroughs, emotional highs. But more often, He waits in the stillness, speaking love and clarity that only come when we slow down.

Maybe you've searched for thunder and missed the whisper.

His quiet voice is quietly personal. So don't wait for the dramatic and loud.

God's voice is powerful. It carries the strength to move the mountains within.

Some of the most defining and powerful moments of my life occur in my quiet moments with God — a verse that impresses itself on my heart, a conviction in prayer, or a calm assurance in the dark. That's why we need to step away long enough to hear from God.

For Elijah, the whisper wasn't just comfort — it was an invitation to retreat, to realign, and to remember who he was in God's eyes.

Retreat to Realign

Elijah wasn't restored in the crowds or through another miracle. He was restored alone on Mount Horeb — away from pressure, noise, and expectation.

There, he rediscovered who he was: not just a prophet or a performer, but God's beloved servant — deeply known and deeply loved.

We all need those sacred pauses. We all need moments to step away and let God remind us who we really are.

Here's a question for you. Have you felt the nudge to stop, but resisted — afraid everything might fall apart if you did? What if it's your soul that's unraveling because you won't?

Sometimes the bravest thing you can do is stop.

To be still.

To let God remind you your worth isn't in what you accomplish — but in being His.

I've had to learn this again and again. Seasons when I kept pushing, trying to stay strong — only to find myself coming undone. And in those moments, God gently called me back.

To breathe.

To remember.

That I am not His employee. I am His child.

Every time I've dared to retreat, He's met me there — ready to realign my heart with His.

"Only in silence can the Word of God be heard. And only in silence can it be obeyed." — Dietrich Bonhoeffer

When the noise fades and the stillness deepens, something sacred begins:

The soul softens.

The Word sharpens.

The Spirit restores what life has scattered.

And that's exactly what we see in the life of Jesus.

What God whispered to Elijah in the cave, Jesus lived out every morning — choosing quiet over the crowd.

Jesus Treasured His Quiet Time with the Father

Again and again, the Gospels pull back the curtain on a rhythm in Jesus' life — moments when He stepped away from the press of people and the weight of ministry to be alone with His Father.

"Very early in the morning, while it was still dark, Jesus got up, left the house and went off to a solitary place, where He prayed." — Mark 1:35

"But Jesus often withdrew to lonely places and prayed."— Luke 5:16

"One of those days Jesus went out to a mountainside to pray, and spent the night praying to God." — Luke 6:12

"Then Jesus went with His disciples to a place called Gethsemane, and He said to them, 'Sit here while I go over there and pray.'" — Matthew 26:36

These weren't just strategic pauses.

They were sacred returns.

Even when demands were relentless and the crowds pressed in, Jesus chose quiet.

He chose solitude.

He chose His Father's voice over the roar of public expectation.

Because for Jesus, the Father wasn't just His mission partner — He was His greatest joy.

Prayer wasn't a line on His schedule; it was the place His heart loved most.

Every early morning in the stillness, every lonely hillside under the stars, every garden shadow in the night — all of them were invitations to delight again in His Father's presence.

For Jesus, these moments weren't a break from real life.

They *were* real life.

Everything else — the miracles, the teaching, the healing — flowed from the deep well of love He shared with His Father.

But Why Did He Do This?

Jesus didn't withdraw out of fatigue or habit — He withdrew for relationship.

At the heart of His solitude was something far deeper than discipline: eternal oneness with His Father.

A divine intimacy our mortal hearts can barely imagine —

unbroken, unshaken, alive before the world began.

Rich with love, joy, and mutual delight.

When Jesus stepped away to pray, He wasn't "reconnecting."

He was delighting in what had never been lost.

He was dwelling in the presence that shaped His every step.

The Way of Withdrawal

In a world addicted to noise and urgency, Jesus shows us a better way —

a way of stepping back before stepping in,

of quieting down before speaking up,

of resting deeply before running hard.

Jesus didn't withdraw to escape — He withdrew to realign.

Not because He needed silence,

but because He treasured His Father's voice.

And now, He invites us to do the same —

not to perform,

not to produce,

but simply to be present.

The Daily Rhythm of the Son

This wasn't occasional. It was constant.

Before dawn broke, while the village still slept, Jesus would rise quietly.

Stepping into the cool night air, He would leave the warmth of the fire and the murmurs of sleeping disciples. No crowds. No miracles. No noise.

Just the crunch of His footsteps on the path, the gentleness of the wind in the olive branches, and the presence of His Father.

There, in the stillness, the universe's most important conversation would unfold — not in shouts, but in the quiet cadence of eternal love.

Every miracle, every teaching, every step toward the cross was birthed here, in the quiet hours when only the Father could hear His voice.

"The Son can do nothing by himself; he can do only what he sees his Father doing." — John 5:19

For Jesus, time alone wasn't optional — it was oxygen.

The Garden Before the Cross

And when the road grew hardest, His rhythm held.

On the night He was betrayed, Jesus led His friends out of the upper room, down the slope of the Kidron Valley, into the grove called Gethsemane. Moonlight cut through twisted olive trees as He found His familiar place of prayer.

The weight of the cross pressed on Him like a stone.

The air was heavy with the scent of crushed olives and the nearness of suffering.

He told His disciples, "Sit here while I go over there and pray."

They saw His shoulders sag. They heard His voice tremble.

Falling to the ground, He prayed:

"Father, if you are willing, take this cup from me; yet not my will, but yours be done." — Luke 22:42

This was no casual retreat.

It was the place where intimacy and obedience collided.

In that garden, Jesus chose again what He had chosen in every solitary place before: the Father's will over His own.

Anguish fell from His skin like drops of blood, yet the bond held — unbroken, unshaken.

Why Solitude Mattered

Jesus withdrew to stay aligned — to renew His strength, resist the pull of the crowd, and show that true power flows from communion, not constant activity.

While the crowds clamored for more — more bread, more miracles, more spectacle — Jesus slipped away to stillness.

Because He knew:

Power doesn't come from the crowd.

It comes from abiding.

Get Away to Come Alive

So come.

Step away from the noise.

Find your quiet place — not to escape the crowd, but to hear the whisper that calls you close.

Let your soul breathe again.

Let your heart be still enough to remember: the strength of your life flows from communion with the Father.

This isn't about silence for silence's sake.

It's about returning to the One voice that knows your name, speaks peace, and leads you forward — not with volume, but with presence.

When the crowd roars… follow the cloud.

Because God still whispers.

And those who dare to listen will come alive.

And here's the thing: the whisper isn't just for steady days.

It's for when you can't see ten feet ahead.

Stillness trains your soul for the seasons when the horizon disappears and faith becomes your only compass.

Sooner or later, the fog will roll in.

And when it does, the quiet you've practiced will be your anchor — helping you walk with Christ even when the path has vanished.

That's where we're going next.

If you want the cloud to lead you in the fog, you must first learn to hear it in the quiet.

CLOUD MARKER

**The strength you need tomorrow is formed
in the stillness you choose today.**

Prayer Prompt

Lord Jesus, You never chased the noise of the crowd—you withdrew to listen.

Teach me to do the same.

Quiet what competes within me.

Train my heart to recognize Your whisper.

Give me courage to step away, humility to be still,

and faith to trust that Your presence is enough.

Meet me again in the quiet.

Amen.

Reflection Questions

1. What noise—internal or external—is shaping your thoughts more than God's voice right now?
2. What most competes with stillness in your life: hurry, fear, distraction, or control?
3. When have you felt most connected to God—and what role did silence or solitude play?
4. What would it look like to treat solitude not as escape, but as encounter?

Live It Out

This week, schedule a sacred appointment: **30 minutes of intentional stillness.**

- No noise.
- No screens.
- No agenda—just you and God.

Begin with this prayer: *"Speak, Lord, for Your servant is listening."* Then stay. Let the silence do its work.

Trust this:

The presence you're seeking is closer than the noise you're avoiding.

CHAPTER 9

WHEN THE FOG ROLLS IN

Trusting God when the Path Disappears.

"For we live by faith, not by sight."

— 2 CORINTHIANS 5:7

You don't need to see the whole way when you know the Guide.

A Walk in the Fog

Every now and then, on my early morning prayer walk, I step onto the path along the creek and find it swallowed in fog.

Thick. Still. Quiet.

Landmarks vanish. Trees fade to shadows. Even the sound of the water and birds turns muted, as if the whole world is holding its breath.

I walk slower in the fog. My eyes can't see far ahead, so my ears — and my spirit — sharpen. Every shape in the mist appears first as a silhouette, then slowly resolves into a fellow traveler. Recognition brings relief — not a threat, just someone else finding their way through the same haze.

And in that quiet, I hear it.

Not an audible voice, but a steady pull in my spirit:

Trust Me… even here. Even now.

There's an awareness we obtain in the fog — not of sight, but of faith. When everything else is hidden, God's presence often feels more real.

By the time I climb out of the creek valley, the fog is usually lifting. Light breaks through. The path returns.

But I never forget:

Even when I couldn't see the way, He was walking with me all along.

When Fog Unsettles Us

The Bible doesn't describe "fog" the way we do, but it often speaks of clouds, mist, and thick darkness — moments when God's presence was near, yet unseen. Just like the fog on my morning walks, those moments invite us to trust Him when we can't see what's ahead.

Fog unsettles us. It erases familiar markers, blurs what once felt certain, and turns confident strides into careful steps. In those moments, we crave clarity. We want to see the next turn, the finish line — some assurance we're not lost. But God doesn't always lead with a spotlight and a clear road. Sometimes, He leads us into the fog on purpose.

One of my favorite promises for these seasons is Isaiah 42:16:

"I will lead the blind by ways they have not known, along unfamiliar paths I will guide them; I will turn the darkness into light before them and make the rough places smooth… I will not forsake them."

God doesn't promise to reveal every step — He promises to walk with us. To guide us along unfamiliar paths. To turn darkness into light, one moment at a time.

When the fog rolls in, faith stops being theory. It becomes real. The cloud hasn't vanished — it's come down low, wrapping around us, slowing us to the pace of His whisper. And just like a driver who instinctively eases off the gas when visibility drops, fog forces us to slow down in life too.

We live in a world that prizes speed — progress, productivity, constant motion. But fog interrupts that rhythm. It refuses to be rushed. It invites you to walk, not run… to pause, not push… to linger with God instead of sprinting ahead alone.

Psalm 23 offers that kind of pace:

"He makes me lie down in green pastures, He leads me beside quiet waters, He refreshes my soul." — Psalm 23:2-3

That's not the language of urgency. That's the pace of the Shepherd.

And sometimes, the fog isn't just a metaphor. It becomes a lived experience — one you never saw coming.

That's how it felt when I lost my brother, Damian.

No warning. No time to prepare. Just a sudden, heavy fog that dropped over everything I thought I understood. One moment, I was walking with confidence… the next, I couldn't see at all.

When the Fog Rolls In

Sometimes fog doesn't drift in gently. It crashes in.

Not the soft kind that settles over a creek at sunrise, but the thick, disorienting kind you find on the highway — sudden, suffocating, and impossible to predict. One minute, everything feels clear. The road ahead seems steady. The next? Your visibility vanishes. You're forced to slow down, or stop completely. The world you thought you understood gets swallowed in gray.

I thought I knew what fog felt like — until the day the horizon disappeared in a single phone call.

My younger brother Damian — vibrant, strong, full of life — spoke the words I'll never forget:

"They found cancer in my lungs."

He had never smoked a day in his life. The diagnosis didn't fit. Not medically. Not spiritually. It didn't belong to any of the categories we use to make sense of pain. It didn't match our prayers. It didn't match his life.

I remember gripping the phone like it might anchor me, the silence on the other end loud with unspoken fear. My heart pounded. My mind scrambled for answers. I wanted a framework. I wanted it to make sense. All I got was fog.

Damian wasn't just my brother. He was a force of joy. A worship leader whose voice carried weight — not just musically, but spiritually. He wrote songs sung in churches that never knew his name, but still feel his spirit. His laughter filled rooms. His kindness changed people.

We shared a room as kids. Wrestled on bedroom floors. Stayed up late with windows cracked open even in winter. I always won (I was older), but he never held a grudge. He had that rare mix of conviction and warmth. Everyone loved him.

When the diagnosis came, we did what people of faith do.

We prayed.

We fasted.

We hoped.

We fought.

We met at his favorite prayer spot — a place he called Still Waters. A bend in the Milwaukee River hidden beneath trees, crowned by a small waterfall. It was his sanctuary. It became ours.

There, my brothers and I poured out prayers with open hands and breaking hearts. We asked for healing. For mercy. For time.

The water kept running. So did our tears.

But the fog never lifted.

Test after test. Report after report. Hope chipped away.

And then, just like that... he was gone.

Damian passed at thirty-three, leaving behind his wife, Gail, his two little girls, Jaelyn and Jaeda, and a wake of grief too deep to measure. A family stunned. A community aching. Parents forced to bury their youngest child. Two older brothers — Larry and me, his only sister, Terri, and a host of nieces, nephews, aunts, uncles, cousins, and friends, all suddenly trying to figure out how to move forward without him.

I remember driving home from the funeral, my sons in the back seat, their faces pressed against the windows, silent tears streaming down their cheeks. We didn't speak. We couldn't. The fog wasn't just outside — it was inside us.

And then came the voice I didn't expect.

A few days later, I was driving Damian's daughters — just four and six. His oldest looked up from her car seat, her voice barely a whisper:

"Uncle Daryl, God answered our prayers. Daddy is healed now… in heaven."

The Ache That Stays

I could barely respond then.

And as I write these words now—years later—I still can't.

God was present then.

And God is present now.

But so is the ache.

Grief is strange like that. It doesn't travel in a straight line. It doesn't wrap up cleanly. It lingers. It waits. Sometimes it hides—until the light shifts—and then it ambushes you all over again.

I didn't fall apart when Damian died—not all at once.

I kept moving.

Kept leading.

Kept praying.

But something inside me went quiet.

I told myself I was being strong. Maybe I was. But sometimes what looks like strength is just sorrow in disguise—a weight we're too afraid to name.

Even now, I don't think I've fully let myself feel it all.

Not long ago, my mother found some old cassette tapes of Damian preaching. Neither of us had heard his voice in over twenty years.

I wasn't sure I was ready to listen.

I wasn't sure I could survive the sound of his voice.

So we decided to listen together. Maybe we could carry the sorrow if we carried it side by side.

I held the cassette recorder for a long time. My fingers hovered over the button, my chest tight—as if pressing play might break something open I couldn't control.

Then I pressed play.

And there he was.

It didn't destroy me.

But it did something else.

It cracked something open.

Grief rushed in—but so did God.

Because some fog doesn't lift all at once.

Some fog thins slowly—over decades, not days.

And some days, the fog rolls right back in.

No warning.

No apology.

But what I've learned—slowly, painfully, tenderly—is this:

Even then… God is still there.

He doesn't wait for the fog to clear before He comes looking for us.

He moves toward us in it.

He meets us in the ache we've been afraid to feel.

He doesn't rush us.

He walks with us.

I'm still learning to trust Him there—not only when the road is visible, but when my heart is clouded too.

Because healing isn't the absence of pain.

It's the presence of God in the middle of it.

And honesty?

That's where healing begins.

Presence Over Understanding

Some fog lifts. Some linger.

Some questions grow quiet with time. Others stay — not loud, just steady — like a slow ache beneath the surface.

After Damian died, I didn't get answers. I didn't get closure.

I got silence. I got ache.

And I got a Presence that refused to walk away.

"When you pass through the waters, I will be with you; and when you pass through the rivers, they will not sweep over you." — Isaiah 43:2

That promise didn't keep the waters from rising.

It kept them from drowning me.

Over time, I stopped chasing answers and started learning how to recognize nearness.

I stopped asking, "Why did this happen?"

And started asking, "Where is God in this?"

And the answer, again and again, was: right here.

Not standing on the shore shouting instructions — but stepping into the deep with me.

Maybe you're in deep waters right now.

Maybe you're tired of pretending you're fine.

Maybe you've been holding your breath for a long time, trying not to feel the full weight of what you've lost.

If so, let this next truth steady you:

You're not alone in the fog.

And you're not the only one who's walked through it.

The Fog Finds Us All

The fog doesn't pick favorites.

You can be faithful.

Prayerful.

Wise.

Grounded.

And still — it comes.

The call you weren't expecting.

The diagnosis that doesn't make sense.

The loss that leaves you breathless.

The silence that settles in and refuses to budge.

Fog doesn't mean you've failed.

It doesn't mean God has gone silent.

It just means you're human — and you're living in a broken world that doesn't always offer clean answers.

Even Jesus — perfect, sinless, divine —

wept at the tomb of His friend.

groaned in Gethsemane.

carried sorrow as deep as any soul has ever known.

If He wasn't exempt from fog… we won't be either.

But here's the good news:

Fog isn't just where we lose our way.

Sometimes, it's where we learn how to follow.

It strips away our self-reliance.

It silences our formulas and fixes.

It invites us to walk, not by certainty, but by trust.

That's what God's people have always done.

Not just when the path was clear — but when it vanished.

They followed a pillar of cloud through the wilderness.

They walked through parted seas and prison cells and unanswered prayers.

And in every step, they were never alone.

If you're not in a foggy season right now, one day you will be.

And when that day comes — or if that day is already here —

you don't need to panic.

You don't need to pretend.

You don't need to have it all together.

You just need to stay close to the One who's already holding you.

And that's where we'll go next.

If You're in the Fog Now

Maybe your story doesn't look like mine.

But the ache? The disorientation? The questions that feel too heavy to carry?

That part might feel all too familiar.

Maybe your fog looks like this:

- A job that ended before you were ready
- A dream that hasn't started, and you wonder if it ever will
- A diagnosis that changed everything
- A relationship that fractured without warning
- A marriage stuck in quiet distance
- A child who is drifting
- A financial pressure that keeps tightening its grip
- A quiet weight of depression, anxiety, or loneliness no one else sees
- A season of waiting that feels endless, with no relief in sight
- A loss that still sneaks up and breaks your heart all over again

If any of that resonates — or if you're in your own version of fog — I want to speak this over you:

You are not failing.

You are not forgotten.

You are not lost.

Even if you can't see the next step.

Even if you feel too tired to take it.

Even if all you can do is sit in the silence and breathe.

God sees you — and He's not going anywhere.

He's not frustrated with your pace.

He's not disappointed in your doubt.

He's not startled by your sadness.

He is near.

Nearer than your fear.

Kinder than you expect.

Stronger than what's coming against you.

And while the fog may blur your view, it hasn't blurred His.

He sees the whole path — and He's still leading you, one grace-soaked step at a time.

So take the pressure off.

You don't need a polished plan.

You don't have to put on strength you don't feel.

You just need to stay close.

Keep breathing.

Keep praying — even if they're messy.

Keep trusting — even when it feels fragile.

Because the fog may hide the road ahead —

but it can't hide you from the Shepherd who never lets go.

Not in the sunlight.

Not in the storm.

Not in the fog.

You are still held.

Still seen.

Still being led.

Anchor Scriptures for Foggy Days

When everything feels unstable, you need something that doesn't move.

Not just a verse to memorize — but a truth to lean on.

These are promises you can grip when your strength is gone.

They're not bandages.

They're anchors.

Blood-bought.

Battle-tested.

Always true.

For those who follow the cloud.

1. *You Are Not Alone*

"Never will I leave you; never will I forsake you." — Hebrews 13:5

The fog may say, *"You've been left."*

It may try to convince you that God has stepped away, that He's not paying attention, that you're walking this road in the dark by yourself.

But the truth is stronger than the fog.

God has not moved.

Not for a second.

You are never alone — not in the confusion, not in the fear, not in the moment you feel like you can't take another step.

Even when you can't hear Him, He's listening.

Even when you can't see Him, He's holding you.

Even when the silence feels endless, His presence has never wavered.

You are not forgotten.

You are not abandoned.

You are not invisible.

The Shepherd who called you by name is still walking right beside you — steady, faithful, and closer than your next breath.

2. *This Will Not Be Wasted*

"And we know that in all things God works for the good of those who love him, who have been called according to his purpose." — Romans 8:28

Right now, this may not feel good.

It may feel wrong, unfair, or unbearable.

It may not make sense for years — and some parts may never make perfect sense this side of heaven.

But God is not wasting a single tear, a single prayer, or a single moment of what you're walking through.

He is weaving something eternal through what feels unendurable.

He's shaping something in you — and through you — that could not be formed any other way.

You may not see the pattern yet.

All you may see is the pain.

But the same God who holds the thread sees the whole design.

And one day — maybe in this life, maybe in the next — you will see what He saw all along:

It was never meaningless.

It was never wasted.

Not one moment.

Not even this one.

3. He Will Finish What He Started

"He who began a good work in you will carry it on to completion until the day of Christ Jesus." — Philippians 1:6

The fog you're in does not cancel God's plans for you.

The delays you didn't choose do not erase the calling He placed on your life.

Your doubts — as real and loud as they may feel — cannot undo His hand at work in you.

The same God who began this story is still writing it.

He hasn't lost His place.

He hasn't changed His mind.

He hasn't walked away in frustration.

What He started in you, He will finish — not halfway, not reluctantly, but fully.

Faithfully.

Beautifully.

You may not see the ending yet, but He already does.

And when it comes, it will be exactly what He intended — perfect in His timing, complete in His purpose, and filled with His glory.

4. His Grace Will Carry You Through

"My grace is sufficient for you, for my power is made perfect in weakness." — 2 Corinthians 12:9

You may be exhausted.

You may feel like you've reached the end of yourself — no strength left, no answers left, no fight left.

But grace isn't something you have to stockpile in advance.

It shows up in the exact moment you need it.

Not late. Not lacking. Not once.

You don't have to hold yourself together by sheer willpower.

You don't have to pretend you're strong when you're not.

You simply have to lean into Him — the One whose strength has no limit.

He's not waiting for you to prove you can handle this.

He's offering to carry you through it.

And when your own strength runs out, you'll find His hasn't even begun to fade.

These truths don't just live on pages —

they live in the lives of those who've walked through fire and found God faithful.

They are not poetic ideas.

They are promises from a Father who cannot lie.

So when your feelings fail you, let these truths carry you.

When your footing slips, let these verses hold you steady.

When the questions return, let this be your reply:

"I may not know how this ends…

but I know who's walking me through it."

If You're Not Sure What You Believe

Maybe you've made it this far through the chapter —

and you're not even sure what you believe about God.

You don't know how to pray.

You're not certain if faith still fits.

You just know something in you is reaching — for peace, for meaning, for something real.

If that's you, I want you to hear this as clearly as I can say it:

God is not waiting for perfect faith.

You don't have to get cleaned up before you come close.
You don't have to untangle all the theology.
You don't have to pretend to be sure.
God honors honest reach more than polished religion.

"God did this so that they would seek him and perhaps reach out for him and find him, though he is not far from any one of us." — Acts 17:27

He's not far — not from the doubter, the struggler, the skeptic, or the one hanging by a thread.
He's not offended by your questions.
He's not threatened by your uncertainty.
He's moved by your hunger — even when you don't know what to call it yet.

"The Lord is close to the brokenhearted and saves those who are crushed in spirit."— Psalm 34:18

So if you're confused, hurting, or just not sure where to begin, you're not disqualified.
You're the reason grace exists.
You're exactly the kind of heart Jesus moves toward.

Take a Step Toward God

You don't need a perfect prayer.
You just need an honest one.
Here's one you can pray right now — wherever you are:

A Prayer from the Fog

God,
I don't have it all figured out.
But I know I need You.
The fog feels heavy, and I want to find You in it.
If You're real, would You show me?

If You see me, would You speak to me?
I bring questions. I bring pain. I bring need.
But right now, I open my heart.
Lead me — even if it's just one small step.
Amen.

This is only the beginning. Keep seeking Him — because in doing so, God promises you will find Him:

"Ask and it will be given to you; seek and you will find; knock and the door will be opened to you. For everyone who asks receives; the one who seeks finds; and to the one who knocks, the door will be opened." — Matthew 7:7–8

When Light Breaks Through

You may not feel different yet.
The fog may still linger.
The silence may stretch longer than you hoped.
But hear this:
This is not the end of your story.
God is not finished with you —
not in the waiting,
not in the wrestling,
not in the wondering.
In Scripture, breakthroughs rarely happened in the spotlight.
They happened in caves, deserts, prisons, and storms.
They happened in hidden, quiet places.
So if you feel hidden,
maybe you're not being overlooked…
maybe you're being *formed*.
Rooted. Protected. Prepared.
One day — not by magic, but by mercy — the fog will lift.
And when it does, you'll see:
God was never absent. He was intentional.

You weren't being buried.
You were being planted.
So walk slowly, if you must.
Breathe. Whisper. Trust.
Even here — even now — the light is breaking through.

Keep Walking Forward

The fog may have blurred your path —
but it hasn't dimmed your calling.
It may have slowed your pace —
but it hasn't stopped God's plan.
Because we don't live by clarity.
We live by **faith**.

"For we live by faith, not by sight." — 2 Corinthians 5:7

So, here's your quiet courage for today:
The fog may linger.
But your Father does too.
And that is enough.
Take the next step.
Breathe again.
Keep going.
You're not lost —
you're being led.
And even now —
even here —
the light is coming through.

CLOUD MARKER

**You don't have to see the way forward when you
trust the One who walks beside you.**

Prayer Prompt

God,

When the path ahead feels hidden, remind me that You are not.

When I feel lost, anchor me again in Your nearness.

Give me the courage to keep walking—not because I see the way,
but because I trust the One who is with me.

Slow my pace to match Yours.

Draw me close, and teach me to live by faith, not by sight.

Amen.

Reflection Questions

1. Where in your life do you feel surrounded by fog right now—
   uncertain, disoriented, or weary?

2. What would it look like to release the need for clarity and
   practice deeper trust instead?

3. What Scripture can serve as an anchor for you when answers
   don't come quickly?

4. Who near you may also be walking through fog—and how can
   you walk beside them with patience and hope?

Live It Out

This week, take one simple step of faith—even if the outcome remains
unclear.

Write **2 Corinthians 5:7** where you'll see it each day:

"For we live by faith, not by sight."

Let it remind you:

- You are not behind.
- You are not alone.
- You are not forgotten.

You are being guided—even in the fog.

PART THREE

WHEN TRUST BECOMES SURRENDER

EVENTUALLY, TRUST ASKS something of us.

Not just belief.

Not just endurance.

But surrender.

This final part moves from formation to response. From being held by grace to being sent by it. Here, faith becomes visible. Decisions are made. Crowns are laid down. Towels are picked up. And the God who led His people out now sends them forward.

Obedience is not the absence of fear—it is the choice to move despite it. And it is always grounded in grace. Grace that catches us when we fall. Grace that gives us courage to rise. Grace that turns followers into servants and servants into witnesses.

The journey does not end with clarity.

It ends with commissioning.

The cloud still moves.

And now, you are invited to go.

CHAPTER 10

NO MAP, JUST GOD

Trusting His Character When the Lie Says Take Control

*"Trust in the Lord with all your heart and lean not on your
own understanding; in all your ways submit to him,
and he will make your paths straight."*

— PROVERBS 3:5-6

God doesn't promise us a map — He promises us Himself.

IN THE LAST chapter, we saw how faith keeps moving when the path disappears. Faith doesn't need a floodlight on the whole journey; it needs steady reliance on the One who walks with us through the fog.

But when the fog lingers, the temptation shifts. The longer the waiting stretches, the more we feel the pull to stop trusting and start taking control.

This is where dependence on God stops being an idea and becomes a lifeline. We crave certainty because it feels safe. We want the plan mapped out, every turn marked, every route guaranteed. Beneath that craving is the deeper pull — the desire to stay in control. We convince ourselves, *If we just knew everything ahead of time, we'd trust quicker and obey sooner.* But God doesn't call us to perfect visibility. He calls us to complete reliance, the kind of confidence that steadies us when the way is hidden, and the wait feels endless.

And here's the deeper truth: uncertainty doesn't only test our patience, it exposes what we really believe about God. Is He good? Is He wise? Is He enough? Or are we still quietly trusting ourselves to take control of the future?

Belief — Where Many Begin but Few Continue

Picture yourself in a hospital room. The diagnosis is fatal unless you go under the knife. The surgeon stands ready — years of training behind him, every tool prepared to save your life. You could repeat all day, *"I believe this surgeon can heal me."* But nothing changes until you stop resisting, lie back on the table, and let the anesthesia take over. That's the moment belief becomes trust.

Scripture makes the same distinction. James refuses to blur the line:

"Faith by itself, if it is not accompanied by action, is dead." — James 2:17

"You believe that there is one God. Good! Even the demons believe that — and shudder." — James 2:19

Jesus said the same to those who had a superficial belief:

"To the Jews who had 'believed' him, Jesus said, 'If you hold to my teaching, you are really my disciples. Then you will know the truth, and the truth will set you free.'" — John 8:31–32

Did you catch it? They had "believed," but Jesus pressed further: real disciples don't stop at agreement — they remain. They cling. They obey.

And Hebrews drives the point home by recalling Israel's story:

"And to whom did God swear that they would never enter his rest if not to those who disobeyed? So we see that they were not able to enter, because of their unbelief." — Hebrews 3:18–19

Israel didn't lack evidence — they had walked through walls of water and eaten bread from the sky. What they lacked was trust.

And the testimony is the same from Genesis to Jesus: faith never stopped at belief. It moved when He spoke. It clung when everything else gave way.

Belief says, *"I know He can save me."*

Trust lies down on the table.

Trust lets the Great Physician work.

And this difference is not a minor matter. Jesus made it plain:

"Not everyone who says to me, 'Lord, Lord,' will enter the kingdom of heaven, but only the one who does the will of my Father... Then I will tell them plainly, 'I never knew you.'" — Matthew 7:21, 23

The evidence was clear.

They called Him "Lord," but they didn't live as if He were.

Their words claimed allegiance.

But there was something about their lives that didn't show it.

To confess Jesus as Lord is not a one-time plea of convenience — it is a daily surrender to let Him rule.

Faith that saves obeys.

Love that's real yields.

Trust that's true follows.

Anything less ends in a shocking verdict. And this warning is not cruelty but mercy. God speaks plainly, so no one is deceived into standing before Him with a faith too shallow to save.

Faith Defined in the Scriptures

From beginning to end, Scripture never separates belief, trust, and faith. In English, we often treat them as different ideas, but in the New Testament they share the same root. *Pistis* speaks of faith — the settled confidence of the heart. *Pisteuō* means to believe or to trust — that confidence lived out in action: entrusting, obeying, relying. In Scripture, faith is never something you merely hold — it's something you lean on, rely on, and live.

"Now faith is confidence in what we hope for and assurance about what we do not see." — Hebrews 11:1

Faith is not wishful thinking. It is lived reliance on God — a trust that keeps moving even when the road disappears. Not because works replace faith, but because true faith refuses to stay still.

If you trust a bridge, you walk across it — even when fog hides the other side. That's why Peter stepped onto the waves, not because water could hold him, but because Jesus could. Paul called it *"the obedience of faith"* — Romans 1:5.

This has always been true. In the Old Testament, faith wasn't abstract — it was survival. And the Hebrew words themselves demand movement, dependence, and surrender:

- **'Aman** (אָמַן) — the root of *amen*. To believe meant to be held steady. Abraham staked his entire future on God's promise — and it held.

  *"Abram **believed** ['aman] the Lord, and he credited it to him as righteousness."* — Genesis 15:6

- **Chasah** (חָסָה) — to run for refuge, to hide your life in God. David prayed this from the caves while hunted by Saul.

  *"The Lord is my rock, my fortress, and my deliverer; in him I **take refuge** [chasah]."* — Psalm 18:2

Together, these words show faith as anything but theoretical. It steadies when everything tilts. It gives courage when danger closes in. It becomes refuge when there is nowhere else to run.

And what steadied Abraham, Daniel, and David steadies us now. From Genesis to Jesus, faith has never been mere agreement in the mind — it has always been trust with the whole life.

It leans.

It moves.

It follows.

Whosoever Believes

Now we come to the most famous verse in the Bible:

> *"For God so loved the world that he gave his one and only Son, that whoever believes in him shall not perish but have eternal life."* — John 3:16

Once you understand that belief is more than mental agreement, this verse strikes differently. John never meant *believe* as a casual nod. He made that clear just a few verses later:

> *"Whoever believes in the Son has eternal life; whoever **does not obey** the Son shall not see life, but the wrath of God remains on him."* — John 3:36 (ESV)

Side by side, the picture is clear:

- Belief → eternal life
- Does not obey → no life

The Greek word translated "does not obey" is *apeitheō*. At its core, it means **to refuse to be persuaded**—and by extension, to resist or reject rightful authority. That's why English translations vary. Some render it "disobey" (ESV, NASB), others "reject" (NIV), and still others "believe not" (KJV).

But the point is the same: unbelief is not neutral. It is active resistance to Jesus. To refuse to believe Him is, at the same time, to refuse to obey Him.

For John, belief and obedience are never two separate roads. They are one path. Belief is not mere agreement; it is **relational trust**. To believe is to trust Christ enough to follow Him. Anything less is admiration dressed up as faith.

That means John 3:16 is not a slogan to memorize but a summons to trust. To believe is to depend—and true dependence always moves toward obedience.

This does **not** mean we are made right with God by meritorious works. Salvation is not earned. But the kind of belief Jesus describes is never passive or indifferent. It is a belief willing to be persuaded—and once persuaded, willing to follow.

That's why I often find myself praying the apostles' words: *"Lord, increase our faith"* (Luke 17:5). When challenges rise and doubt tugs at my soul, that prayer anchors me again—because true belief is always **trust in motion**, not mere mental agreement.

Eden: The First Breach of Trust

From the beginning, the story of God and humanity has been about trust.

Eden was flawless. God's presence was as close as breath. Every need was met, every desire pure. At the center stood one boundary — not to restrict life, but to guard it.

Then came the serpent. He began with suspicion:

"Did God really say…?" — Genesis 3:1

And when that seed took root, he pressed further:

"You will not certainly die… you will be like God." — Genesis 3:4–5

The lie was simple: *God is holding out on you. If you want what's best, you can't wait on Him — you must take it for yourself.*

In that moment, obedience looked like limitation. Freedom looked like control. Trust gave way to suspicion. And the same whisper still lingers: *God's way is too narrow. His timing is too slow. His goodness can't be trusted.*

So we reach for what seems good instead of trusting the One who is good — and regret meets us there.

But restoration begins differently: by remembering that God can be trusted. He isn't withholding good. His ways remain best. Real life is never found in replacing Him, but in relying on Him.

And history proves it — that whisper from Eden didn't vanish. It rose at Sinai. It echoed in Israel's kings. It surfaced in the early church — even in Peter by a fire. And it still lingers now.

The High Cost of Compromise

Every collapse in Scripture follows the same thread: **trust fractured, and hearts reached for something other than God.**

- **In the wilderness — impatience turned to idolatry.** While Moses lingered on the mountain, Israel built a calf they could see and touch (Exodus 32:1–6).
- **In the palace — desire turned to sin.** David, who once sang psalms under the stars, stayed behind in idleness. Temptation came, and he took what wasn't his (2 Samuel 11:1–27).
- **In the early church — image turned to hypocrisy.** Ananias and Sapphira wanted the honor of sacrifice without the surrender it required (Acts 5:1–11).

The pattern is unmistakable: Israel traded faith for sight. David traded devotion for desire. Ananias traded truth for image. And beneath it all was the same whisper: ***"You can't fully trust Him — take control yourself."***

When Cravings Take Control

And if we're honest, the pattern shows up in our lives too. Addiction may look different — a bottle, a screen, a pill, a secret habit — but the lie underneath is the same: *"This will satisfy you. You can control it. God isn't enough."*

Addiction is just another way we try to seize control when trust feels too costly. We tell ourselves; *I need this to cope, I need this to feel alive, I can quit whenever I want.* But the truth is, the moment we bow to that craving, that craving begins to control us.

Scripture names it clearly:

"All of us also lived among them at one time, gratifying the cravings of our flesh and following its desires and thoughts."— Ephesians 2:3

That's what being enslaved to our flesh really is — following cravings instead of following Christ. And every collapse — ancient or modern — begins with the same whisper: *God can't be trusted. Take control yourself.*

But Paul doesn't leave us there. He lifts our eyes to the only hope that breaks the chains.

"But because of his great love for us, God, who is rich in mercy, made us alive with Christ even when we were dead in transgressions — it is by grace you have been saved." — Ephesians 2:4–5

Our flesh says, *You'll never be free.*
Grace says, *You already are alive in Christ.*
Our cravings shout, *You'll always need me.*
God whispers, *My mercy is enough.*
And I know that whisper well — because the battle with impulses of the flesh hasn't just lived in Scripture or in other people's stories. It's lived in all of our stories, including mine.

The Fall That Taught Me to Trust

The cracks that ran through Israel ran through me too. They showed up in quiet seasons — when discouragement drowned out God's promises.

As I said earlier, I grew up in church, eager to honor Christ with purity. But in college, those cracks widened into crevasses, and I faltered. My first tears came not from godly sorrow but from shame — until conviction finally cut deeper than regret.

During that season, anger smoldered inside me. Frustration grew into outbursts, and one day it erupted on the basketball court. A fight left me with a broken hand — and the heavier break of explaining to people who thought of me as "spiritual" why my arm was in a sling. It's one thing to lose your temper; it's another to walk into church with the evidence visible for all to see. Outwardly, I looked fine; inwardly, I was unraveling.

Looking back, it wasn't lust or anger alone that undid me — it was weakened *Pistis*. Each failure carried the same invitation: His whisper — *Daryl, believe and depend on Me.*

The real battle wasn't just against my flesh — it was about trust. Trusting God's goodness when I didn't feel good. Trusting His sufficiency when I felt empty. Trusting His way when I couldn't see the ending. Trusting His plan over my own.

> *"Trust in the Lord with all your heart and lean not on your own understanding; in all your ways submit to him, and he will make your paths straight."* — Proverbs 3:5–6

That verse became my compass, pointing me back to God when pride and self-sufficiency had me wandering. Those falls exposed my need for His mercy, compassion, and faithfulness.

Another verse became like oxygen in my lungs: *"My grace is sufficient for you, for my power is made perfect in weakness."* — 2 Corinthians 12:9

Grace unlocked me. Steadied me when I wanted control, strengthened me when surrender felt impossible, and trained me to resist lies before they took root:

> *"We take captive every thought to make it obedient to Christ."*
> — 2 Corinthians 10:5

That's where the real battle lives — at the thought level. Sin whispers, *"You'll never overcome this."* If I let that lie linger, despair grows. But when I answer with truth — *"His power is made perfect in weakness"* — the spiral breaks. Not by my will, but by His Spirit.

Following the cloud isn't one grand decision. It's a daily choice to trust, to surrender again and again. Not because I hold the map — but because I have the Guide.

Every fall showed me the same truth: I don't need the map. I need the Guide.

The God You Can Trust

When God revealed His name to Moses, He wasn't handing over a title — He was unveiling His very character:

> *"The LORD, the LORD, the compassionate and gracious God, slow to anger, abounding in love and faithfulness, maintaining love to thousands, and forgiving wickedness, rebellion and sin. Yet he does not leave the guilty unpunished..."* — Exodus 34:6–7

Compassionate and gracious — His kindness meets us where we are.

Slow to anger — His patience carries us through failures we thought would finish us.

Abounding in love and faithfulness — His promises hold steady when everything else shakes.

Forgiving wickedness and sin — He welcomes us back from every betrayal.

Yet He is **just** — the guilty are not ignored, and **His holiness will not be mocked.**

This vision of God shatters the old lies from Eden to today: *Is God really enough? Will His way satisfy? Can His timing still be trusted?* We grab control and chase counterfeits when we forget who He is. But when we see Him clearly, trust stops being optional — it becomes the only sane response.

We stop compromising because we already have the treasure we're tempted to steal. Real dependence says: *Even if it doesn't make sense, even if it costs me dearly, I believe You are who You say You are — and You are enough.*

To acknowledge Him is not a polite nod toward heaven but the surrender of every hidden place — our decisions, our relationships, our ambitions, our battles. His love and faithfulness will guide us far better than our limited understanding ever could.

And the promise still stands: He will make your paths straight. Not always easy. Not always quick. But always sure. Always guided. Aligned with His best.

So start now. Open your hands each morning and pray:

"Lord, today I choose to depend on You completely — because You are who You say You are."

Will You Trust?

This is the invitation.

Not to silence your questions,

but to trade the illusion of control for the security of His presence.

When uncertainty presses in, the pull will be strong:

Grab the wheel. Cut the corner. Reach for what feels safer than surrender.

Don't.

That path looks steady, but it only breeds more fear.

The better way is trust.

You won't always get it right — but one choice can change everything:

"Trust in the Lord with all your heart."

The same God who carried you through the fog stands beside you now.

Compassionate. Gracious. Faithful. Enough.

So lay down the blueprints.

Release the lie that you must see every turn before you take the first step.

Lean into the One who already knows the way.

Not the map, but the Guide.

Not control, but trust.

His presence is the certainty.

And control? Always the counterfeit.

Maps will fail you.

Control will betray you.

But the Guide never does.

Prayer Prompt

Lord, I confess that I often crave certainty more than I seek Your presence.

I want the plan before I yield my heart.

Teach me to surrender every hidden corner—

to trust You not only with my beliefs, but with my obedience.

When fear pulls me toward control, remind me of who You have revealed Yourself to be:

compassionate, gracious, faithful, forgiving, and just.

Form deeper dependence in me.

Teach me to trust You because of Your character, not my circumstances.

Amen.

Reflection Questions

1. What areas of your heart still resist God's full authority?
2. Where are you tempted to believe lies about God's character instead of resting in His truth?
3. How can you actively depend on God's revealed character—compassionate, gracious, faithful, forgiving, and just—this week?
4. What is one concrete step of obedience God is inviting you into right now?

Live It Out

This week, write out **Proverbs 3:5–6** or **Exodus 34:6–7** and place it where you'll see it daily—mirror, dashboard, lock screen, or desk.

Each time you notice it, pause and pray aloud:

"Lord, I trust You—not because I see the plan, but because I know Your heart."

Let this become a rhythm, not a slogan.
Return to it when fear surfaces or control feels safer than trust.
At the end of the week, journal:

- where trust felt costly,
- how obedience tested you,
- and how God met you in the surrender.

CHAPTER 11

THE NET BENEATH THE FOG

How Grace Catches You and Gives You Confidence

"Though he may stumble, he will not fall, for the
Lord upholds him with his hand."

— PSALM 37:24

Grace is the net beneath your calling.

The Safety Net That Changed Everything

They called it "the bridge that couldn't be built."

In the early 1930s, the Golden Gate Strait had swallowed more than its share of ships and dreams. The winds were vicious. The fog was blinding. The water churned cold and merciless. Still, San Francisco dared to imagine a span of steel connecting its shore to the Marin headlands — 200 feet above the bay.

The risk? Almost certain death.

In that era, one fatality per million dollars spent was expected. With a $35 million price tag, the Golden Gate Bridge was assumed to cost dozens of lives.

Every day, men stepped onto narrow beams with nothing but sky below. A single misstep — a slip in the wind, a dropped rivet — could send them plunging to their deaths. They moved slowly. They moved scared. And who could blame them?

Maybe you've walked like that, high up on the thin beams of faith, with the wind of fear in your ears, afraid one wrong move might end it all. Maybe you've been in a season where you weren't sure you could keep your footing.

Then Chief Engineer Joseph Strauss made a radical decision: install a massive net beneath the bridge. The price tag? $130,000 in the middle of the Depression — over $2.5 million today. Critics scoffed. Some called it weak. Others, wasteful. But Strauss believed human lives were worth the cost.

It worked.

Nineteen men fell — and lived. They called themselves the "Halfway to Hell Club."

But something else happened.

The work accelerated. The crew walked with confidence. Fear loosened its grip. Productivity soared — not because the danger vanished, but because they knew even if they fell, they wouldn't be lost.

The net didn't remove the risk.

It removed the despair.

And that net? It's more than a construction marvel.

It's a picture of grace. Costly. Scoffed at. Radical.

The Golden Gate net cost a fortune for its time, but it was nothing compared to the price of our safety. Grace didn't come cheap — it cost heaven the blood of Christ. Critics mocked. Some still call it weakness. But the cross is God's declaration that you are worth the cost. That's the gospel.

That's why you can walk with confidence.

Not because the danger has vanished, but because even if you fall, you won't be lost.

The First Sermon I Ever Preached

I was fifteen when I preached my first sermon.

It was a Wednesday night at the church on Mandrake Road in Madison, Wisconsin. Sam, our minister, had noticed how I leaned in during youth group, how I kept asking questions. One night, he pulled me aside and said, "Daryl, I want you to preach a midweek message — to the whole church."

I tried to act cool, but inside I was spinning. Nervous. Shocked. Excited.

The first thing I did was call my grandmother in Milwaukee — "Gang Gan," we called her. She and my grandfather had always dreamed that their grandsons might become preachers. When I told her, she didn't hesitate: "That's great, baby! I've got the perfect sermon for you."

Three days later, a manila envelope arrived. Inside was a neatly typed sermon titled *The Grace of God,* based on Ephesians 2:1–10. Eight points. The first line read: *Grace is unmerited favor.*

I didn't fully understand it, but I knew it mattered. For two weeks, I studied and practiced. When Wednesday came, I stepped behind the pulpit — a nervous teenager with a pressed shirt and sweaty palms — and read it word for word. Seven minutes later, I was done.

The church was kind. The youth group loved it — mainly because it meant they got outside sooner. But what stayed with me wasn't the polite applause or the brevity. It was the message.

Back then, grace was doctrine. A definition. Unmerited favor, a point on a page.

When Grace Becomes Personal

The sermon Gang Gan mailed me wasn't just for the church that night. It was for me — for every future moment I'd fall short, feel unworthy, or wonder if God could still use me.

Now I know what I didn't then: grace is the net beneath the fog. The safety that catches you when you stumble. The reason you can rise again when shame says stay down.

Maybe that's where you are.

Maybe you've tried to keep walking in faith… but the fog rolled in.

Maybe you've fallen — hard.

Maybe you're still haunted by what you did or didn't do.

Maybe you're afraid you've blown it for good.

If that's you, hear this — not from me, but from the Word of God:

"Though he may stumble, he will not fall, for the Lord upholds him with his hand." — Psalm 37:24

"Therefore, there is now no condemnation for those who are in Christ Jesus." — Romans 8:1

You might have slipped. But if you belong to and trust in Christ, grace is still beneath you — alive, present, and powerful enough to hold you and call you again.

The same grace that saved you at the start still holds you now. It doesn't mean you won't stumble. It means you don't have to stay down.

So take a breath.

The net is in place.

And the One who built it isn't finished with you yet.

Grace Is Who He Is

That sermon came from one passage: Ephesians 2:1–10.

Those verses are not just theology. It's a rescue story.

"As for you, you were dead in your transgressions and sins…" (v.1)

Paul doesn't say we were limping or lost — he says we were dead. Spiritually lifeless. Deserving wrath.

Then come two of the most hope-filled words in Scripture:

"But God…" (v.4)

But God, rich in mercy, made us alive with Christ — even when we were dead. It is by grace — charis, a gift, a lifeline — that we've been saved.

And that mercy didn't start with Paul. It began in Exodus 34, right after

Israel's Golden Calf disaster. If there was ever a time for God to start over, that was it. Instead, He revealed His core identity:

> *"The Lord, the Lord, the compassionate and gracious God, slow to anger, abounding in love and faithfulness..."* (v.6)

This is the same God from Genesis to Revelation. Grace didn't suddenly appear when Jesus was born — it's who God has always been. He didn't set aside justice to show mercy; He satisfied them both in Himself.

What began at Sinai was completed at the cross.

The mercy that passed before Moses in the cleft of the rock is the same mercy that raised you from death — and still holds you when you fall.

Grace Is the Net That Holds Because God Doesn't Let Go

Ephesians 2 isn't just about *how* we're saved — it's
about *who* saves us.

It's not the story of a distant deity reaching down once from heaven.

It's the story of the God of Exodus 34 — the same One who led by fire and cloud, who walked among His people in mercy and power — stooping down again and again to pick us up when we couldn't stand.

> *"It is by grace you have been saved... and this is not from yourselves, it is the gift of God."* — Ephesians 2:8

Not earned.

Not deserved.

Freely given.

That's the net.

That's why you can move again after you fall — not because you're strong, but because God is faithful. Not because you're guiltless, but because He is gracious.

Here's what we forget: God knew we would fall.

He didn't install the net *just in case* we slipped.

He placed it there because He knew we would.

That's the testimony of Scripture: not that *some* miss the mark, but that *all* do.

"For all have sinned and fall short of the glory of God." — Romans 3:23

That "fall short" means to miss the target — to step off the edge and come up short of the standard.

Not once. Not by accident. But consistently. Universally.

We've all fallen off the bridge:

- Some by pride.
- Some by fear.
- Some by rebellion.
- Some by exhaustion.
- Some were pushed by trauma or betrayal.
- Some slipped quietly. Others crashed spectacularly.

The outcome is the same: we fall.

And yet — grace was already there.

The net doesn't appear after you cry for help. It's been stretched out from the start — anchored to the character of the God who knew your weakness and still chose to walk with you.

Grace doesn't deny your fall.

It refuses to let your fall be the end of your story.

Paul Got It

Paul knew what it meant to fall — and fall hard.

Before he ever wrote about grace, he ran from it.

Before he proclaimed the gospel, he persecuted it.

Before he built churches, he tore them apart.

Then Jesus stopped him cold on the Damascus Road.

Blinding light. A voice from heaven. Truth he couldn't outrun.

In an instant, everything Paul trusted in collapsed — his résumé, his self-righteousness, his moral superiority. He didn't just lose his sight; for the first time, he *saw* who he really was: flawed, fallen, failing.

"Christ Jesus came into the world to save sinners — of whom I am the worst." — 1 Timothy 1:15

Not "was" — *am.*

That wasn't shame. That was truth.

Paul finally saw the gap between his goodness and God's holiness.

He knew no performance could close it. And he knew — at last — that grace was the only net strong enough to prevent him from falling.

The cross became his rescue — not just as history, but as his personal lifeline. It was where God's justice was satisfied and God's love displayed, at the same time.

That's why Paul could write with such conviction. Grace didn't just save him; it changed him. And when doubt whispered or the weight of his past pressed in, he remembered Jesus' words:

"My grace is sufficient for you, for my power is made perfect in weakness." — 2 Corinthians 12:9

Not in strength.

Not in self-confidence.

In weakness.

Paul got it.

And when we get grace — *really* get it — God gets us. We don't just receive forgiveness; we receive fuel, identity, and the courage to get up and keep going.

Because the net is still there.

And Paul's story isn't just something to admire — it's something to step into. We've all had our Damascus Road moments. Maybe not with blinding light, but with blinding regret — moments when we finally see how far we've fallen.

Sometimes grace meets us right there.

Other times, we wonder if it still will — especially when the fog we're in is our own fault.

When the Fog Is Your Fault

Sometimes the fog in life comes from circumstances we can't control.

But sometimes? We caused it.

We said the words, clicked the link, told the lie, ran ahead.

Now we feel disoriented — not because life is unfair, but because sin leaves a haze.

And the hardest part to admit?

We knew better. We did it anyway.

Then comes the fear:

Maybe I've ruined everything.

Maybe this time grace won't catch me.

Maybe I've worn it out.

So we hide.

We stall.

We sabotage the calling God gave us — not because He quit on us, but because we quit on ourselves.

But you're not the first to blow it.

Not the first to fall hard.

Not the first to create your own fog.

Ask Peter. Ask David. Ask Paul.

Their sins were massive, public, devastating — and yet none of them outran the grace of God. Neither can you.

The fog may be your fault — but the net is still there.

Not because you deserve it, but because God refuses to let go.

He doesn't say, *"Earn your way back."*

He says, *"I still want you."*

He doesn't demand you rebuild before you return.

He reaches down and says, steady and sure, *Let's begin again — together.*

What the Spirit Wants You to Hear

You don't just stumble — you fall short.

And no matter how hard you try, you can't close the gap.

You are more broken than you'd ever admit…

and more loved than you could ever imagine.

But here's the wonder: God doesn't recoil at your weakness.

He doesn't ration out mercy or hesitate with forgiveness.

From Sinai's fire to Calvary's cross,

He has always been the same — compassionate, gracious, slow to anger, abounding in love.

And grace is anything but cheap.

It cost God everything.

Justice wasn't brushed aside; it was carried.

Holiness wasn't compromised; it was satisfied.

At the cross, Jesus stood in your place.

You were caught by grace because He was crushed by wrath.

When that truth takes hold, the gospel stops feeling like theory and starts breathing like life.

The fog begins to lift.

The net beneath your failure no longer feels symbolic — it feels solid.

Real. Stretched tight under every step you take.

You don't just know about grace.

Grace knows you.

And it will not let you go.

The God who built the net isn't waiting to see if you'll fall,

He already knew you would. And He made sure it would hold.

And this God of Grace doesn't just hold you up when you fall,

He reshapes the way you live.

If you've really been caught by grace, you can't keep it to yourself.

The same net that steadied your steps is the net God now asks you to hold for someone else.

When Grace Catches You, Pass It On

Jesus once told a story about a servant who owed his king an impossible debt — ten thousand talents, more than he could repay in ten lifetimes. The king took pity, canceled the debt, and set him free.

But that same servant walked out and found a fellow servant who owed him a few hundred denarii — a tiny fraction compared to what he'd just been forgiven. Instead of mercy, he grabbed him by the throat and demanded payment. When the man begged for patience, he refused and threw him into prison.

When the king heard about it, he was furious:

> *"You wicked servant! I canceled all that debt of yours because you begged me to. Shouldn't you have had mercy on your fellow servant just as I had on you?"* — Matthew 18:32–33.

The parable is a mirror.

How can we, forgiven an eternal debt we could never repay, withhold forgiveness from someone who wronged us?

How can we fall into the net of God's grace and then refuse to hold the net for others?

Grace that stops with you isn't grace at all. It's wasted.

Real grace doesn't just catch you — it transforms you.

It loosens your bitterness.

It bends your heart toward mercy.

It teaches you to forgive as freely as you've been forgiven.

If you've been caught, pass it on.

Hold the net for the next person.

Offer the mercy you received.

Extend the forgiveness you didn't deserve.

That's the mark of someone who truly knows grace.

And that's the power of the gospel: grace never stops with one person.

It spreads. It multiplies.

It pulls people out of despair and restores them to life.

The Halfway to Hell Club — and the God Who Went All the Way

The nineteen men saved by the Golden Gate Bridge net gave themselves the name the Halfway to Hell Club because they'd fallen, but they didn't die.

Suspended above death, caught by something they didn't deserve.

But grace goes further.

Jesus didn't just stop us midair.

He went all the way — into sin, into wrath, into death, into the grave — so we could go all the way into life.

The net beneath you is stained with blood.

Not bought with rope or rivets, but with love.

You don't just belong to the Halfway to Hell Club.

In Christ, you belong to the Fully Redeemed Family of God.

You were caught — but you were also called.

Back to purpose.

Back to grace.

Back to movement.

So don't freeze.

Don't let shame hold you.

Don't believe the lie that your fall disqualified your future.

The fog doesn't change your calling.

Falling doesn't mean it's finished.

The God who caught you will not let you go.

As Psalm 37 says: *"Though he may stumble, he will not fall, for the Lord upholds him with his hand."*

That's your promise. That's your net.

So move forward. Step out of the shadows.

Take the next step, even if you're trembling.

Because His hand is still extended.

His grace is still enough.

And your story isn't over.

The net didn't remove the risk.

It removed the despair.

And grace — costly, relentless, unbreakable — will always do the same.

You don't need to fear the fall anymore — the cross already caught you.

CLOUD MARKER

Grace is the net beneath your fall and the voice that calls you forward.

Reflection Questions

1. What failure or fall still lingers in your memory, and how does grace speak to it now?
2. Where in your life have you stopped moving because shame convinced you that you're disqualified?
3. Can you name a moment when grace not only caught you— but sent you forward again?
4. Who in your life most needs the same grace God has already shown you?
5. Which part of God's revealed character (Exodus 34:6–7; Ephesians 2:4–9) do you most need to remember right now?

Live It Out

Identify one place where shame still whispers, *"You're too far gone,"* or one relationship where forgiveness still feels costly.

Underneath it, write:

"Grace caught me. God still calls me. And His grace through me can catch others too."

Then take one step forward this week—even if it feels uncertain or unfinished.

Make the call.
Release the grudge.
Ask for help.
Open the Scripture.
Confess honestly.
Forgive freely.
Try again.
Not because you're strong.
Not because you're ready.
But because you are held.
The net is already in place.
The fog does not cancel your calling.
Move anyway.

CHAPTER 12

GRACE THAT MOVES YOU TO FOLLOW

How Discipleship Is Grounded in Grace

*"After this, Jesus went out and saw a tax collector by the name of
Levi sitting at his tax booth. 'Follow me,' Jesus said to him, and
Levi got up, left everything, and followed him."*

— LUKE 5:27–28

Grace isn't just what catches you when you fall —
it's what gets you moving.

The Net That Got Them Moving

You remember the story.

The wind. The steel. The fog.

Hundreds of feet above the water, the men worked suspended between
risk and reward, with nothing to catch them if they slipped.

In the last chapter, we talked about the net—the bold innovation that
saved lives and calmed fears. Grace, we said, is like that net: steady, unseen,

always underneath you. It catches you when you fall. It holds you when you can't hold yourself.

But this chapter isn't about the net's safety. It's about what the net *started*.

Because once the net was installed, everything changed.

The crew didn't just feel protected—they felt empowered.

They didn't just stop fearing death—they started building faster.

Fear had made every beam a battlefield. But now something new filled the air: confidence.

Men moved. They climbed. They took initiative. They reached farther. Productivity soared over 25%.

Why?

Because the presence of the net didn't make them careless.

It made them courageous.

They didn't retreat. They didn't freeze. They advanced.

The net didn't just protect them—it propelled them.

Starting with Fear, Finishing with Grace

Fear can wake you up, but it can't move you forward. And spiritually, the same thing is true.

"The fear of the Lord is the beginning of knowledge." — Proverbs 1:7

Fear of judgment. Fear of being lost. Fear of wasting your life.

That kind of fear can jolt you awake long enough to look toward God—but it can't keep you walking with Him.

That was true for me. One of the earliest reasons I became a Christian was simple: I didn't want to go to hell. I feared facing God unprepared. But fear, on its best day, can only draw a boundary. It can tell you where not to go; it can't teach you how to live.

Fear asks, "How close can I get without crossing the line?"

Grace asks, "How far can I go to please the One who rescued me?"

It wasn't until I began to understand grace—really understand it—that my faith found momentum.

Fear kept me cautious; grace made me courageous.

Fear kept me from slipping; grace taught me to follow.
Fear may wake you up, but grace is what gets you going.
Grace doesn't just catch you when you fall.
Grace sends you forward.

Grace Frees You to Follow Him

Grace isn't a soft-landing place.

It doesn't make you timid or cautious.

It wakes you up on the inside.

It gives strength to your steps and desire to your heart.

Grace gives you the freedom to move, to rise, to follow.

When Paul wrote to the church in Colossae, he said:

"This gospel is bearing fruit and growing throughout the whole world—just as it has been doing among you since the day you heard it and truly understood God's grace." — Colossians 1:6

That line has penetrated my heart every time:

"Since the day you heard it… and truly understood God's grace."

Something happened when they understood.

Their faith didn't stall.

Their repentance didn't freeze.

Their discipleship didn't plateau.

They grew.

They bore fruit.

Their lives took on momentum.

I once heard a preacher say, "You weren't saved to sit. You were saved to serve."

And that's what the believers in Colossae embraced.

They stepped into surrender.

They followed with intention.

Their faith showed up in the way they lived.

Because when grace finally lands in the heart, it changes your posture.
You stop dragging your feet.
You stop hesitating at the edge of obedience.
You stop standing still.
You move.
You follow.
You grow.
Grace releases you.
I can testify to this truth: when grace gets inside you, passivity dies.
I've lived this.
The seasons when grace finally sank past my head and into my heart
— those were the moments I stopped drifting.
My faith didn't stall.
My devotion didn't shrink.
Grace pulled me forward when everything in me wanted to stay where
it was.
That's what grace does.
It wakes you up.
It puts strength in your steps and surrender in your spirit.
Some treat grace like a loophole or a license —
a spiritual permission slip to relax conviction.
Paul shut that down quickly:

"Shall we go on sinning so that grace may increase? By no means!"
— Romans 6:1–2

That question doesn't rise from a heart that understands grace.
It comes from a heart that has missed grace entirely.
Grace never leads you to ask,
"How close can I get to sin?"
Grace moves you to ask,
"How completely can I give myself to Christ?"
And this is where legalism tries to creep in.
Legalism whispers: *Do more. Try harder. Impress God.*

It guilts you into obedience.

It shames you into performance.

It doesn't transform you — it tightens you.

Here's the truth:

Legalism has never produced holiness.

It only produces people who have learned to pretend.

Legalism manages appearances.

Grace transforms the heart.

Legalism creates spiritual actors.

Grace creates surrendered disciples.

Legalism exhausts you with performance.

Grace frees you with presence.

Legalism says, *"Work for God so He won't leave you."*

Grace says, *"God came close — now walk with Him."*

Duty can drag you to the altar,

but only grace keeps you there —

willing, joyful, surrendered.

When mercy truly grips you,

it doesn't loosen your convictions —

it sets them on fire.

It doesn't make you reckless.

It makes you relentless.

Grace doesn't weaken holiness.

Grace fuels it.

Grace doesn't lower the bar.

Grace lifts you to it.

When grace gets in you, everything changes.

You stop performing and start pursuing.

You stop posing and start obeying.

You stop managing sin and start walking in freedom.

Because grace doesn't pamper you —

grace propels you.

When the Fire Fades

Over the years, I've seen passionate disciples burn out.

Not because they stopped believing—

But because they stopped growing.

They didn't grow in their knowledge of Christ.

They didn't deepen their grasp of grace.

And so their fuel ran dry.

Their fire was doused.

Their obedience became routine.

Their calling got buried under self.

People who once said,

"I'll go anywhere, do anything, give up everything for God,"

Now live quietly for themselves—

Sidelined by wounds, weariness, or drifting priorities.

What happened?

Their religion was fueled by duty,

By human accountability,

By tradition,

By fear,

By a hunger for prosperity,

By selfish ambition—

But not grace.

Grace is the only fuel that lasts.

In Chapter Eleven, we saw grace as the net beneath the fog.

But this chapter is about how that same net becomes your launchpad.

And it's what will sustain you for the long haul.

Experiencing God's mercy soothes the broken; it sends the willing.

And in this chapter, we'll begin where discipleship always begins—

Not with effort, but with the grace-filled call of Jesus: *"Follow me."*

Because when grace is real,

It doesn't just change your status.

It changes your steps.

And that's exactly what happened to Levi. For the next several chapters,
we will lean on his example to help us follow the cloud.

When Levi Found Grace

"After this, Jesus went out and saw a tax collector by the name of Levi sitting at his tax booth. 'Follow me,' Jesus said to him, and Levi got up, left everything and followed him."— Luke 5:27–28

He sat behind the table like he did every day.

Coins clinked. Scrolls rustled. Eyes avoided him.

His name was Levi—and he was a tax collector.

That meant he had power—but not respect.

Wealth—but not welcome.

Familiarity with the law—but no access to the temple.

In the eyes of his people, he was a traitor.

To the religious elite, he was unclean, untouchable, unredeemable.

Tax collectors weren't hated just for what they did—but for how they did it, and who they did it for.

Rome taxed everything: travel, trade, harvests, livestock—even personal income.

But instead of collecting directly, Rome outsourced the job to local Jews—men willing to betray their own for profit.

They paid Rome up front, then squeezed extra from their neighbors to make it back—with interest.

They were legalized thieves in a broken system.

Spiritually despised. Banned from synagogues.

Lumped in with prostitutes and pagans—sinners by profession.

Levi wasn't just one of them—he was stationed in Capernaum, along a bustling trade route between Galilee and Roman outposts.

Constant traffic. Constant tolls. Constant opportunity to take more than what was owed.

People knew his face. And they hated it.

He didn't just represent Rome.

He represented everything they had lost: dignity, freedom, and justice.

He wasn't just sitting at a booth—

He was sitting in a reputation.

A compromise.

A hardened role—maybe for survival, maybe for gain—

but now it had become his identity.

That booth was his prison.

And in some twisted way, it had become his shelter.

There's a kind of comfort in compromise when it pays well.

A kind of numbness that convinces you you'll never be anything else.

But that wasn't the whole story.

Levi had another name: **Matthew**—

The name he would later use to introduce himself to the world.

The name under which he would write the first Gospel of the New Testament.

It means "gift of God."

But on this day, at this booth, he didn't feel like a gift.

He felt like a disappointment.

A man with a comfortable income and a bankrupt soul.

Until Jesus showed up.

When grace is real, you don't sit still— you set the table.

> *"Then Levi held a great banquet for Jesus at his house, and a large crowd of tax collectors and others were eating with them."* — Luke 5:29

Levi didn't need a discipleship class to tell him what to do next.

He didn't need to be told to go share the Gospel.

He just knew—*this can't stay with me.*

So he opened his door, filled his house, and gave Jesus the seat of honor.

This wasn't just hospitality. It was testimony.

He didn't just walk away from the booth.

He walked into a mission.

Because when grace finds you like that—you move.

And maybe, as he prepared that banquet, setting the table with nervous hands and a heart still catching up to what had just happened, maybe these words pulsed inside him:

"They're never going to believe this.

Jesus came for me.

He saw me. Spoke to me. Chose me.

Me—the tax man. The traitor. The cheat.

I don't know what's next... but I know this:

I'm not keeping this to myself."

"I've spent years collecting from people.

Now I want to start giving back.

I've spent too long sitting alone behind a booth.

I want to fill my house with people who need what I just found."

And who did he invite?

The only people who would come.

Other tax collectors. Sinners. People with reputations like his.

People with scars they didn't know how to explain, and shame they didn't know how to shake.

And now they were sitting at his table.

Eating. Laughing. Watching Jesus.

Wondering if maybe this grace could be for them, too.

Because Levi said yes.

Mercy and service spread.

This wasn't just dinner—it was discipleship on day one.

The Gospel had started to bear fruit in him, just like Paul described:

"Just as it has been doing among you since the day you heard it and truly understood God's grace."— Colossians 1:6

Levi heard it.

Levi understood it.

And Levi got going.

Grace Offends the Earners
Luke 5:30–32

"But the Pharisees and the teachers of the law who belonged to their sect complained to his disciples, 'Why do you eat and drink with tax collectors and sinners?'

Jesus answered them, 'It is not the healthy who need a doctor, but the sick. I have not come to call the righteous, but sinners to repentance.'"

The music was still playing. The food was still warm. The room was still buzzing with surprise and laughter.

But outside, the religious voices started whispering—

and then complaining.

"Why would He eat with them?"

"Why would He dignify this?"

"Doesn't He know who these people are?"

To them, this was unthinkable.

A rabbi shouldn't be reclining at a table with tax collectors.

He shouldn't be sharing bread with thieves, frauds, and sinners.

He should be at the temple, not at Levi's house.

But they didn't understand what Jesus came to do.

And they certainly didn't understand what grace came to break.

Because **grace always draws criticism from those still trying to earn what Jesus gives away.**

Jesus Didn't Just Call Levi — He Defended Him
Jesus didn't apologize for being there.

He didn't quietly slip away or try to explain the optics.

He spoke. Boldly. Publicly.

"It is not the healthy who need a doctor, but the sick."

He wasn't just defending Himself—He was defending Levi's inclusion.

His table.

His new identity.

His right to belong.

"I have not come to call the righteous, but sinners to repentance."

He made it clear:

Levi *wasn't the problem.*

He was the point.

Jesus came for men like him.

Not in spite of his past—but because of it.

This moment wasn't an exception to Jesus' mission.

It was the mission.

When grace sits down, shame has to leave.

Imagine Levi sitting there, hearing those words.

Jesus had already called him—but now He was **claiming him.**

Publicly. Unashamed. Without qualification.

"He knows who I am… and He still came to my house."

"He knows what I've done… and He still calls me His."

"Let them whisper. Let them judge. I know who sat at my table."

This is what grace does.

It interrupts the shame others expect you to carry.

It confuses the categories religion tries to maintain.

And it defends the dignity you forgot you ever had.

That dinner became more than a meal.

It became a movement—the beginning of a new kind of discipleship, shaped not by performance, but by presence.

From the Booth to the Gospel

Levi didn't just follow Jesus that day.

He followed Him for the rest of his life.

And that man—once known for sitting behind a booth, extorting his neighbors, and carrying the weight of disgrace—would go on to write the very Gospel that bears his new name:

Matthew.

The first book of the New Testament.

The one that begins with a genealogy and ends with a commission.

The one that records the Sermon on the Mount, the parables of the kingdom, and the Great Commission itself: *"Go and make disciples of all nations…"*

Imagine that.

The man once known for collecting taxes…

became the man who recorded the teachings of the Messiah.

Grace caught him.

Grace called him.

And grace kept him going—until the story of Jesus became the story he told.

We will explore more about Matthew in the coming chapters.

When Grace Came for Me

I preached about grace when I was fifteen.

I stood behind a pulpit, Bible open, voice steady, and told people that God forgives. That Jesus saves. That grace is greater than sin.

And I believed it—at least the idea of it.

But back then, grace was something I could explain before it was something I had experienced.

It was true to me. It just wasn't personal yet.

It wasn't until my early twenties that grace stopped being a sermon point and started becoming my lifeline.

That's when I began to see it—the distance.

The distance between who I wanted to be and who I actually was.

The distance between my sinfulness and God's goodness.

And the more that gap stretched, the more I realized:

I didn't just need to preach grace.

I needed to be rescued by it.

I was the religious guy on the team.

The one who never missed church.

The one who knew his Bible.

The one who led devotionals.

The one others looked to as an example.

And yet—I was the one who needed grace the most.

There were nights I'd lie in bed, heart heavy with guilt, and wonder:

"If I died right now… would God actually take me back?"

I'd sinned so blatantly. So knowingly. So repeatedly.

And I started to believe the lie that I had crossed a line God wouldn't erase.

I knew God so loved the world.

I even knew God loved me.

What I doubted was—did God *like* me?

Could He enjoy someone who had failed this hard?

That's what pride does.

It convinces you you're too good to need grace—

until you fall far enough to fear you're too bad to receive it.

But God, in His mercy, began to open my eyes.

Not all at once. Not in dramatic fashion.

But slowly. Quietly. Kindly.

He showed me that grace wasn't just for the rebellious kid on the run.

It was for the Bible kid too.

For the one who had performed his way into approval and was now quietly suffocating under the pressure to keep it up.

He showed me that Jesus didn't wait for me to put the pieces back together.

He came to me in the wreckage.

And that's when it started.

Grace didn't just catch me.

It moved me.

It stripped away the masks.

It broke the grip of shame.

It softened my heart in ways no rule or role ever had.

I had preached about grace before I understood my need for it.

But once I did?

It didn't just change my theology.

It changed my posture.

Because when I finally saw that Jesus didn't just love me—but actually *liked* me—even at my worst?

That's when grace stopped being a net beneath my feet…
and became wind in my lungs.
That's what grace did for me.
And that's exactly what it did for Levi.

And Now—You

Maybe you've known about Jesus for a long time.

Maybe you've grown up in church. Maybe you've even preached a few sermons like I did.

But somewhere along the way, you settled into the booth.

The booth of pride.

The booth of performance.

The booth of shame.

The booth of self-reliance.

And maybe you've started to believe that grace is for everyone else.

Or that you've fallen too far for it to still be for you.

But friend—**Jesus sees you.**

Not just the version you want others to see.

Not the cleaned-up image or the spiritual résumé.

He sees *you.*

And still, He says:

"Follow me."

That's grace.

It's not *"Get it together."*

It's not *"Prove you're serious."*

It's not *"Work your way back."*

Just:

"Follow me."

That's what Jesus said to Levi.

That's what He whispered to me.

And that's what He's saying to you.

Grace is still calling.

And it's not calling you to sit still—it's calling you to move.

To step out of the booth.

To step away from the weight.

To step into the presence of the One who goes before you.

Because this is what it means to follow the cloud.

You don't always get clarity.

You don't always feel ready.

You don't always have a plan.

But when you hear His voice, you go.

You don't need to see the whole horizon—just the movement of the cloud.

When it rises, you rise. When it moves, you move. That's how trust walks forward.

Jesus isn't asking for perfect people.

He's calling willing ones.

And really—this is what this book has been about all along.

Not following a formula.

Not following the crowd.

But following the cloud.

Following the God who still speaks, still leads, and still calls us forward by grace.

So if you hear Him calling you today—don't just believe in Him.

Follow Him.

Not tomorrow.

Not when it's convenient.

Not when you feel holy enough.

Now.

Today.

Accept the grace that gets you going and keeps you going.

This isn't just the end of a chapter — it's your moment at the booth.

The place where Jesus stops, looks you in the eye, and says, "Follow me."

You've followed the cloud this far.

Now let grace move you.

The road ahead may not be easy, but it will be worth it.

Don't settle for the safety of staying seated.
Push back from the table.
Leave the coins behind.
Step into surrender.
Say yes to the God who still calls disciples —
one booth, one banquet, one bold move at a time.

CLOUD MARKER

Grace does more than save you—it moves you.

Prayer Prompt

Jesus,

Thank You for seeing me clearly and still saying, *"Follow Me."*
Thank You for calling me before I was clean
and loving me before I was confident.
Help me believe that grace isn't only for my past—
it's for who I am now
and for who You are shaping me to become.
Break the lie of pride that says I don't need You.
Break the lie of shame that says You wouldn't want me.
Give me the courage to step away from what keeps me stuck
and the endurance to keep walking when I feel tired, discouraged, or
afraid.
I don't want to just admire You.
I want to follow You.
Wherever You lead.
Even when I don't feel ready.
Amen.

Reflection Questions

1. What "booth" are you still sitting in—where pride, shame, or fear has kept you stationary?
2. What do you sense Jesus calling you away from—and where is He inviting you to walk next?
3. Do you believe Jesus not only loves you, but wants you with Him right now? Why or why not?

Live It Out

This week, take one honest step toward Jesus from where you are—not from where you wish you were.

Maybe it's confessing what you've been hiding.

Maybe it's releasing guilt you've carried too long.

Maybe it's opening your table—like Levi did—so others can encounter the grace that found you.

Don't wait to feel worthy.

Don't wait to feel ready.

When grace calls, readiness is not the requirement.

Willingness is.

Step up.

Grace will keep you going.

CHAPTER 13

YES, COMPLETELY YES

You Can't Follow the Cloud and Keep Your Crown

*"In the same way, those of you who do not give up everything you
have cannot be my disciples."*

— LUKE 14:33

Following Jesus starts with a yes—but it continues
with surrender, one step at a time.

The Cloud Keeps Moving

Levi's yes at the tax booth was bold — but it was only the beginning. Grace got him going. But following Jesus? That would take more than one yes.

After the banquet, Jesus slipped away to a mountainside. All night He prayed, alone with the Father. By dawn, word spread: today He would choose twelve from the larger crowd to carry His mission forward.

Levi's pulse quickened as he drew near. What must it feel like to know the Rabbi had spoken your name before the Father through the night? Excitement rose — but so did fear. He wasn't just any follower. He was the tax collector. The one who had sold out to Rome. The one people still whispered about.

Would Jesus really call him? Or would silence prove that grace had limits?

Then it happened. Jesus lifted His eyes and said, *"Matthew."*

Levi's chest tightened when he heard Jesus call him *"gift of God,"* for that is what Matthew means. His eyes stung. Relief and awe rushed over him. Chosen. Called. Seen. The night of prayer ended with his name on the list.

But then he looked to his left… and his stomach dropped.

Simon the Zealot Was on the List, Too

"…James son of Alphaeus, Simon who was called the Zealot…"
— Luke 6:15

Levi barely had time to savor his own name before Jesus spoke another: *"Simon… the Zealot."*

The word hit like a hammer. Levi's stomach knotted. His pulse spiked. He knew what it meant. Simon wasn't just another follower — he had once carried the dagger of Israel's most feared movement, men sworn to drive out Rome with blood. To Rome, terrorists. To many Jews, heroes. But to tax collectors? Executioners.

And now Jesus had spoken his name in the same breath as Levi's.

Levi could almost feel his stare — sharp, burning, cutting through him. To Simon, he was the traitor who had fattened himself on Rome's silver while his people suffered.

Yet Jesus called them both. Out loud. In public. Into the same circle, on the same mission. The yes was before them — not just to leave their old lives, but to step into it together.

What kind of kingdom was this? One that placed a tax collector beside a Zealot. One that bound a betrayer of Rome's taxes with a betrayer of Rome's peace.

The tension must have been electric. Levi had laid down his booth. Simon his blade. And now Jesus was asking for more: their identities, their allegiances, their very selves.

Because in the kingdom of God, old identities die. Old allegiances break. Old crowds dissolve. When Jesus said, *"Follow me,"* He wasn't just calling them out of their pasts — He was calling them into something entirely new.

Luke 9:23-26
The Yes That Costs Everything

"Then he said to them all: 'Whoever wants to be my disciple must deny themselves and take up their cross daily and follow me.'" — Luke 9:23

The choice was set before them. Levi had heard his name. Simon had heard his. Both had to decide: would they step into the yes — or step away?

And Jesus made sure they knew exactly what that yes would cost.

He didn't quietly mention this part.

He didn't reserve it for the inner circle.

He didn't pull the Twelve aside and say, *"Okay, now that you're all-in, here's the deeper stuff."*

No — He said it to them all.

Everyone listening. Every man. Every woman. Every would-be disciple, then and now.

"Whoever wants to be my disciple…"

Not whoever wants to be a church leader.

Not whoever wants to go into ministry.

Not whoever wants to take their faith "to the next level."

Whoever.

You. Me. The Twelve. The crowd. The modern churchgoer. The new believer. The skeptical seeker.

To be a true follower of Christ, a disciple of Jesus, is not a specialty track. It's the only track.

Deny Yourself

The circle grew still as Jesus' voice cut through the mountain air. Levi and Simon weren't the only ones with a choice that day — every person in the crowd had to decide. And so do we.

"If anyone wants to be my disciple…" I can see Jesus' eyes sweep across the crowd's faces — fishermen and farmers, skeptics and seekers, tax collectors and zealots. No one was excluded.

Then He said it plainly: *"You must deny yourself."*

Not indulge yourself. Not affirm yourself. Not "be true to yourself." Deny yourself.

It's saying, I no longer trust myself to lead myself. I step aside so Christ can take over.

Too many nominal believers and churchgoers today miss this; we often shrink what Jesus said down to something small — skipping dessert, powering through the gym, trying harder. But what Jesus calls us to is deeper. It's surrendering your will when it collides with His Word. It's giving God the final say when your feelings fight your faith. It's silencing pride when it demands the spotlight. It's refusing to let comfort or convenience become your god.

To deny yourself is to take off your crown and lay it at His feet. It's surrendering the throne of your own life. It's saying, in those moments when your flesh demands, *"Satisfy me,"* — *I am not king anymore. Jesus is.*

And here's the truth: it never gets easier. Every Jesus follower can testify that the same sharp pain it took to lay down their will at the start is the same sharp pain it takes today. For me, after decades of seriously following Jesus as Lord, my flesh desires are still familiar — to be right, to protect my image, to chase comfort, to be selfish, to guard my ego. They haven't gone away. Following Jesus still means choosing, moment by moment, to say no to me and yes to Him.

Ministry tests my selfishness.

Living in a broken world tests my selfishness.

Various relationships test my selfishness.

It calls me to lead with faith when I'd rather coast in ease.

And I know the future will demand the same. New seasons. New costs. New crosses.

But I welcome the struggle. Because every painful *no* to myself becomes a deeper *yes* to Jesus. Every crown I lay down makes room for His. And every surrender pulls me closer to His heart.

Take Up Your Cross Daily

"Whoever wants to be my disciple must deny themselves and take up their cross daily and follow me." — Luke 9:23 (NIV)

Everyone in the Roman world knew what a cross meant. It wasn't jewelry. It wasn't a metaphor. It was a death sentence. When a man picked up a cross, he was walking to his own excruciating execution.

And Jesus told them to carry one—every day.

To die to pride and self-centered ego.

To die to the applause and approval of people in favor of God.

To die to the need to be right.

To die to the impulses of the flesh that pull you away from Christ.

To die to whatever keeps you from following the cloud.

This isn't weekend-only Christianity. This is daily surrender. Daily obedience. Daily death to self so Christ can live through you.

What does that mean for us? It means saying no to pride on Monday, not just singing about humility on Sunday. Resisting compromise on Thursday afternoon, not just nodding along to a sermon once a week. Choosing forgiveness when bitterness rises on Wednesday; choosing integrity when temptation calls on Friday; choosing surrender when fear presses in on Saturday.

Taking up your cross is not an event. It's a daily way of life—a daily decision to say yes—completely yes.

Follow Me

Then Jesus gave the invitation: *"Follow me."*

Don't just believe in Me. Follow Me.

Where I walk — walk. Where I stop — stop. Where I lead — go.

This is different than raising your hand in a service or saying a quick "salvation prayer." Following Jesus isn't about a moment of emotion — it's about a lifetime of motion. Step by step. Day by day. Surrender by surrender.

You weren't made to blaze your own trail. You were made to follow the cloud.

"For whoever wants to save their life will lose it, but whoever loses their life for me will save it." — Luke 9:24

You can chase your dreams, your image, your platform. You can win the world. But you'll lose your soul.

Jesus isn't interested in rearranging your priorities. He wants to rebuild your life from the inside out.

"What good is it for someone to gain the whole world, and yet lose or forfeit their very self?" — Luke 9:25

The world will applaud your gain and ignore your loss. But Jesus sees it all — and only He can save what the world can never give back.

Luke 14:25-33
When You Say Yes, You Love and Trust Jesus the Most

Take a moment to read Luke 14:25–33. These verses contain some of Jesus' hardest words—and yet they are among the most ignored when it comes to calling people to follow Him. But here, He lays down the terms of discipleship with absolute clarity. In this passage, we can see three main truths that demand our attention.

"Large crowds were traveling with Jesus, and turning to them he said: 'If anyone comes to me and does not hate father and mother, wife and children, brothers and sisters—yes, even their own life—such a person cannot be my disciple. And whoever does not carry their cross and follow me cannot be my disciple.'" — Luke 14:25–27

Jesus never softened His words to keep a following. He wasn't interested in building a fan base. Instead, Christ thinned the crowd because He was making disciples. That's why He often spoke the most brutal truths when the crowds were at their biggest. His call was never about popularity — it was about priority.

The word *"hate"* here was rabbinic hyperbole, a common way of teaching by sharp contrast. Jesus wasn't commanding us to despise our families or ourselves. After all, He commands us to love our neighbors and even our enemies (Matthew 5:43). Jesus instead was calling us to love Him so supremely, so fully, that every other attachment would look like hate in comparison.

Or, as He put it more plainly:

"Anyone who loves their father or mother more than me is not worthy of me." — Matthew 10:37

It's not about removing love for others. It's about reordering it. Jesus doesn't ask for a place in your life — He demands first place. Not a category. A crown. And to say yes is to take that crown off and give it to Him.

This Is What "Christian" Really Means

You can admire Him. You can agree with Him. You can even wear the title "Christian." But unless you trust Jesus to be first, you're not actually following Him.

And that matters — because the first people called Christians weren't casual attendees or cultural affiliates. They were disciples (Acts 11:26). Men and women who had laid down their crowns and surrendered everything to follow the King.

Which means the word "Christian" only makes sense if Jesus is your highest love — not just a name you claim, but a life you live.

The Ultimate Love Test

And Jesus wouldn't leave that claim in theory — He pressed it into reality. It's easy to say He's first when nothing competes for that spot. But what happens when obedience disappoints your parents, offends your kids, or costs you your reputation?

That's the moment of clarity.

Because in that moment, you will choose: the crowd you love — or the cloud you follow.

And Jesus doesn't sugarcoat it: *"Such a person cannot be my disciple."*

Not "should try harder." Not "needs more time." Cannot.

Not because He doesn't want them —

but because they don't actually want Him more than everything else.

The Cost That Comes with The Call

"Suppose one of you wants to build a tower. Won't you first sit down and estimate the cost to see if you have enough money to complete it? For if you lay the foundation and are not able to finish it, everyone who sees it will ridicule you, saying, 'This person began to build and wasn't able to finish.'" — Luke 14:28–30

Jesus wasn't trying to talk people into following Him — He was warning them not to do it lightly. The crowds were swelling, the excitement building. And that's when He stopped, turned, and asked the question most leaders avoid:

"Have you actually counted the cost?"

He painted a picture everyone knew: a half-built tower. Foundation poured. Frame started. Beams rusting. Work abandoned. What began with a vision ended in embarrassment.

That's what He was warning against — not failed effort, but unconsidered commitment.

Because discipleship is costly. We love beginnings — a new job, a new relationship, even a new faith journey. But Jesus isn't impressed by our launches. He's after our finishes. He doesn't want a momentary yes that evaporates under pressure, but a steady yes that endures when it's tested, stretched, and misunderstood.

His message was clear: don't just get excited. Get ready. Because discipleship isn't about passion alone. It's about endurance.

I recall the day I bowed my knee and made a sincere and serious commitment to trust Jesus as my Lord. I had to count the cost. And for me, the first cost was pride. I had worked so hard to polish the image people saw — the outward me that won applause — while neglecting the inner me that God already knew. The real me. The one I couldn't hide from Him.

Following Jesus meant more than scrubbing the surface. It meant surrendering the secret places. Letting Him confront the pride, the ego, the false strength I had built my life on. I remember praying, *"God, I need a new heart. A pure heart. A heart that values truth when no one's watching. A heart of integrity."*

That was my first surrender. The first crown I laid down. And it wouldn't be the last.

Jesus Doesn't Hide the Fine Print

That moment taught me something vital: Jesus never hides the terms. He doesn't lure you in with half-truths and then spring the cost later. He tells you upfront.

Following Him is deeply personal — yes, it's passionate, yes, it's love — but it's also a decision. A counted, costly decision. Faith that begins with emotion must be sealed with conviction. You don't prove discipleship by tears at the altar when everyone is watching; you prove it by carrying your cross when no one is.

Jesus wants us to finish what we begin. He doesn't want us to quit on Him when life hits hard. He is looking long-term for builders. People who dig deep, who pour the foundation, who refuse to quit when the storm hits. People who keep saying yes. Not once. Not occasionally. But every day. For life.

It's All Yours, King Jesus

"Or suppose a king is about to go to war against another king. Won't he first sit down and consider whether he is able with ten thousand men to oppose the one coming against him with twenty thousand? If he is not able, he will send a delegation while the other is still a long way off and will ask for terms of peace. In the same way, those

of you who do not give up everything you have cannot be my disciples." — Luke 14:31–33

Jesus' second parable cuts deeper. Not about building, but about battling. A king weighs his odds and realizes the truth: he's outmatched. He knows the math doesn't work. Ten thousand against twenty thousand. The only wise option left is surrender before the first sword is drawn.

This isn't just a parable. It's a warning.

There's a war coming. A kingdom clash. And you are not the stronger king. Jesus is not the underdog here — He is the King with twenty thousand. He doesn't invite negotiation. He grants you time to surrender. That's not cruelty — it's mercy.

But mercy has an expiration date.

The battle isn't just coming someday — it's already underway. Every day you resist Him, you're already losing ground. The King is still a long way off. But He won't stay that way. And when He comes, every rival kingdom will collapse. Every throne built on pride, pleasure, or self will be shattered under His.

To the One Who Says "Later"

You might think: Exactly. That's why I'm not ready yet.

"I'll get serious later. After I settle down. After I've tasted what I want. After I clean myself up."

But later is a lie. Later is not guaranteed.

You don't negotiate with a King by delay. You don't buy time with excuses. The only path to peace is surrender — now.

Jesus told this story to rattle the procrastinator. To wake the one who says "Not yet." To warn the one who assumes tomorrow is promised.

The King is coming. And when He arrives, the time for peace will be over.

He Sets the Terms — Total Surrender

This King is merciful, but He is not soft. He is patient, but He is not passive. He is love, but He is also Lord.

And His terms are non-negotiable:

"Those of you who do not give up everything you have cannot be my disciples." — Luke 14:33

Not some things.
Not just sinful things.
Everything.
Every right.
Every crown.
Every competing loyalty.
Every false kingdom you've built.

The Question Isn't Whether You'll Bow — It's When

You can bow now — while He is still "a long way off." Or you can bow later — when His army arrives and resistance is crushed. Either way, the end is the same:

"Every knee will bow… and every tongue will confess that Jesus Christ is Lord." — Philippians 2:10–11

The wise king doesn't wait. He doesn't stall. He sends his delegation today. Because when the true King arrives, the time for mercy is gone.

So, What About You?

Matthew didn't delay.

When Jesus passed by his tax booth and said, *"Follow me,"* he didn't negotiate terms. He didn't ask for more time. He didn't clean up his act first. He stood up, left everything, and followed the King.

And he never went back.

Yes, he wrestled.

Yes, he counted the cost.

Yes, he walked beside people who once would've been his enemies. But when Jesus called, Matthew stepped into the yes — not just once, but again and again.

And he grew.

Jesus called him as he was, so that He could guide him step by step — transforming him from tax collector to disciple, and from disciple to Gospel writer. History tells us he penned the very account that still calls people to follow Jesus two thousand years later.

From the booth…

to the banquet…

to the mountaintop…

to the margins of the empire…

Matthew walked with Jesus until the end — because he had already surrendered everything.

He didn't just admire Jesus. He bowed.

And when the dust settles, there will be no half-built towers in the kingdom.

No rival thrones still standing.

No lingering kings clutching their crowns.

There will only be those who said yes — and meant it.

So what about you?

The King is still "a long way off" — but He's coming.

The cloud is still moving — but it won't circle back.

The time for delay is done.

Don't just believe in Him.

Bow to Him.

Follow Him.

Give Him everything.

Because stepping into the yes means stepping off your throne, laying down your crown, and letting Jesus take His rightful place.

That's what Matthew did.

That's what Simon did.

And that's what you're being invited to do — today.

CLOUD MARKER

You can't follow the cloud and keep your crown.

Prayer Prompt

Jesus,

I hear You calling—not just to believe, but to follow.

I confess the things I've held onto:

my comfort, my control, my authority over my own life.

Today, I lay them down.

Take the crown I was never meant to wear.

Take my life. Take my will. Take my future.

Lead me as You led Matthew—

out of what was familiar and into what is faithful.

I no longer want the throne.

I step into the yes and place everything in Your hands.

Amen.

Reflection Questions

1. What have you been most reluctant to surrender to Jesus— control, comfort, security, reputation, or relationships?
2. In what ways have you admired Jesus without fully yielding to His authority?
3. What would obedience that costs you something look like in this season of your life?
4. Have you ever followed Jesus partially, but hesitated when full surrender was required? What would it mean to say yes again?

Live It Out

This week, identify **one specific area** where Jesus has been calling for full surrender—and where you've been holding back.

Name it.

Write it down.

Lay it at His feet in prayer—and then act in obedience.

Tell someone you trust what you are surrendering and invite them to walk with you.

Don't delay.

Don't negotiate.

Say yes today.

And when tomorrow comes—say yes again.

CHAPTER 14

THE TOWEL AND THE TABLE

How Surrender Becomes Service

"The Son of Man did not come to be served, but to serve..."
— MATTHEW 20:28

Your hands can be the ones God uses to answer someone's prayer.

When Your Yes Finds Its Hands

Saying yes to Jesus isn't the end of the journey — it's the beginning of the pouring out.

In the last chapter, we stood at the edge of surrender. We counted the cost. We loosened our grip. We laid down control and said, *"Yes, Lord. Completely, yes. Wherever You lead."*

But here's what we must see:

That yes?

It doesn't just reverberate in heaven.

It reshapes your life here on earth.

That yes doesn't just rise up in worship — it reaches out in love.

It doesn't just live in your heart — it finds its way into your hands.

Because when you follow the presence of God, He will never lead you to comfort without compassion.

He won't stop at spiritual formation and skip over faithful action.

Where God goes, compassion flows.

And if you're truly following the cloud, it will eventually place you face-to-face with someone who's hurting, hungry, overlooked, or forgotten — and it will ask you to kneel.

This may not happen on a platform. It likely won't happen in a spotlight. But it will happen — because that's where Jesus goes. And if you're walking with Him, you will be led to the places where love is most needed.

It might lead you to:

- A child growing up in poverty, unsure if there will be dinner tonight
- A refugee family starting over with nothing but trauma and hope
- A man carrying all he owns in a backpack, still searching for home.
- An elderly widow, invisible to the world outside
- A neighborhood where violence is normal, and opportunity is rare
- A prisoner whose name the world forgot — but whose soul Jesus still pursues
- A mother fleeing abuse with children in tow, searching for safety
- A people group that is still waiting for justice
- An orphaned child longing for a family

Following Jesus means more than agreeing with His words.

It means walking in His footsteps — and His footsteps always led to the least, the last, and the lost.

"Whatever you did for one of the least of these brothers and sisters of mine, you did for me." — Matthew 25:40

But the presence of God won't just lead you to serve *out there.*

It will also lead you to serve *right here* — in your church community.

Because the same Spirit who sends you into the world also places you within the body.

He equips you for mission *and* for ministry.

You were never meant to be a spectator in the Kingdom — not in the world, and not in the church.

You were designed to belong *and* to build.

To reach the lost *and* to strengthen the found.

To bring light into dark places *and* to bring life to your spiritual family.

"To each one the manifestation of the Spirit is given for the common good." — 1 Corinthians 12:7

That means your gifts aren't just helpful — they're essential.

And they're not limited to a platform. They show up in ordinary, everyday faithfulness.

It might look like:

- The prayer you whispered before service
- The smile you gave as a greeter to someone who almost didn't come
- The grass you mowed to keep the grounds beautiful and inviting
- The meal you cooked for a family in need
- The time you gave to shape the faith of a teenager in the youth group
- The dinner you hosted for a small group

- The diaper you changed in the nursery
- The repairs you made to keep the property safe and welcoming
- The tech you ran behind the scenes
- The kindness you showed when no one was watching

It all matters.

It all builds the body.

It all reflects the heart of Christ.

Because the cloud doesn't just lead you to the margins — it leads you to the middle of the community, where mutual service knits hearts together and strengthens the whole.

This is what surrender looks like in motion:

It moves you toward people in pain and toward a church community in need.

It leads you to bear burdens, break bread, build up, and bless — not occasionally, but daily.

Every act of service is more than a task — it's a table being set.

Your faithfulness makes room for Jesus to move.

This is what Jesus meant when He said, "bear much fruit" (John 15).

Fruit isn't just a spiritual feeling — it's visible love. Tangible compassion.

Real action that reveals a real Savior that results in changed lives.

When the presence of God truly fills your life, service becomes your lifestyle.

A Table and a Decision

"Then Levi held a great banquet for Jesus at his house, and a large crowd of tax collectors and others were eating with them." — Luke 5:29

It's one verse. Just one. But don't let the brevity fool you.

This wasn't casual. It wasn't convenient. It was **costly**.

After Jesus called Levi from the booth, he threw a banquet — a *great* one — and that decision changed everything.

Imagine it.

The smell of roasting meat over open flames.

The sound of servants hurrying in and out of the courtyard.

The clatter of dishes, the spilling of wine, the hum of laughter and curiosity.

A table long enough to welcome all the wrong people.

Tax collectors. Sinners. Stragglers. Skeptics.

People who never got invited to the righteous man's table… but who found themselves drawn to the compassion of the only One truly righteous.

And Levi made it happen.

He opened his home — his private space.

He spent his money — food for dozens, maybe more.

He sacrificed his reputation — aligning himself publicly with this rogue Rabbi.

He invested his time — planning, preparing, cleaning, coordinating.

He gave his relational capital — inviting people from his old life to meet the One who just gave him a new one.

And for what? For one reason:

To make room for Jesus to move.

He said yes — and then he served.

Don't miss it:

He didn't lead a Bible study.

He didn't preach a sermon.

He didn't offer theological exposition.

He cooked. He cleaned. He opened the door. He created space.

And that space became sacred.

Because when Jesus enters a room filled with hungry people — physically or spiritually — He doesn't waste the moment.

He calls. He heals. He reveals.

And Levi got to be the one who made the introduction.

That's the heart of a disciple.

That's what service looks like.

It's not always dramatic — but it is always demanding.

It will cost you something — your time, your comfort, your energy, your resources.

But when Jesus has your heart, the table becomes an altar and the towel becomes your joy.

The Servant Way

And Jesus made it clear — Levi wasn't just doing something generous.

He was stepping into something sacred.

Because everything Jesus did, everything He taught, everything He modeled for His disciples pointed to this one truth:

> *"For even the Son of Man did not come to be served, but to serve, and to give his life as a ransom for many."* — Mark 10:45

That one sentence — so familiar, so often quoted — should shake the foundation of how we think about greatness.

The Son of God didn't come to climb ladders.

He came to descend.

To serve. To stoop. To sacrifice.

And He didn't just say it — He showed it.

On the night He was betrayed…

The night when He knew the cross was just hours away…

The night when His disciples were still arguing about which of them was the greatest…

Jesus did something they would never forget.

> *"So He got up from the meal, took off His outer clothing, and wrapped a towel around His waist. After that, He poured water into a basin and began to wash His disciples' feet…"* — John 13:4–5

No spotlight.

No stage.

Just a towel… a basin… and dirty feet.

Feet that had walked long roads.

Feet that had tracked dust and dung and disappointment.

Feet belonging to men who didn't fully understand Him — and one who would betray Him.

And still — He knelt.

He scrubbed.

He served.

And when He was finished, He looked up and said:

"Now that I, your Lord and Teacher, have washed your feet, you also should wash one another's feet... I have set you an example that you should do as I have done for you." — John 13:14–15

This wasn't symbolic. It was formative.

This is what discipleship looks like — in sandals and silence, on your knees, with a towel in hand.

The King stooped.

The Savior served.

The Cloud bent low.

And He calls us to do the same.

Following the Presence Means Finding the Need

This is what happens when you truly allow the Spirit to lead you — not just in worship, but in life.

You'll be led to needs.

Not just global needs — though yes, God may call you across oceans.

Not just dramatic needs — though yes, He may place you in moments of crisis.

But more often?

You'll be led to the kind of needs that hide in plain sight.

- A spouse who feels emotionally invisible and doesn't know how to say it.
- A child who needs your time more than your advice.
- A neighbor whose name you've never learned — but who's walking through quiet grief.

- A coworker who jokes to mask the weight they carry.
- A classmate who's isolated and unseen.
- A friend who says they're "fine" but hasn't smiled in weeks.
- A single parent trying to do it all — and silently falling apart.
- A caregiver who's exhausted and silently begging for backup.
- A boss who leads others but has no one caring for them.
- A stranger at the grocery store who just needs kindness, not correction.

These aren't just *human* needs — they're *holy* invitations.

They're not always loud, but they're always near.

Because the Spirit of God doesn't just call you to the big and obvious — He calls you to the quiet, inconvenient, everyday opportunities that prove whether your "yes" is real.

Discipleship doesn't begin when you're scheduled to serve — it begins when you start paying attention.

Following Jesus isn't about finding a stage or waiting for a title —it's not for the selfishly ambitious.

It's about finding people — and loving them like He would.

And if you're truly following His presence — the cloud that guided Israel… the Spirit who now dwells in you… The Savior who still leads one step at a time — you won't be led to ease.

You'll be led to need.

You'll serve *in the world* — in the tension of injustice, pain, and brokenness.

You'll serve *in your everyday life* — in living rooms and break rooms, driveways and dinner tables, commutes and coffee shops.

That's what discipleship demands.

That we say yes like Levi.

That we serve like Jesus.

When the Towel Is Carried Well

This kind of discipleship isn't theoretical for me—I've seen it lived.

I've watched people I love carry the towel of service with humility, consistency, and joy. Their faithfulness is quiet, but its impact is unmistakable. They don't seek recognition; they reflect the heart of Christ. I want to tell you about a few of them.

My mother, Sharon Reed, is a servant of the soul. Her ministry is encouragement. If you know her, you've likely felt it—a handwritten card, a thoughtful gift, a timely word shaped by prayer. She listens for God's prompting and responds with care. Because her encouragement is so steady, even her occasional words of correction land gently. That's what real service looks like.

My uncle, Michael Avery, serves with strength poured out in love. His hands are never idle, his heart always open. He doesn't just help—he leads through action. If there's a burden to lift, he's already moving. He gives without keeping score, and his life preaches before he ever speaks.

Raynold Mensah, our executive administrator, is the backbone of our local ministry. He carries countless responsibilities with excellence, humility, and calm under pressure—and somehow still finds time to encourage others. He doesn't just keep things running; he helps them flourish. And he does it with joy.

I could go on. Amalie Carr, our faithful administrator, quietly leads a company of behind-the-scenes servants—those who organize, clean, greet, and give—keeping our fellowship steady and strong. Her humility and consistency alone could fill a chapter.

And there are so many more.

Men and women who prepare worship with care.

Who labor so children and students flourish.

Who shepherd others through joy and sorrow.

Who give quietly, consistently, and joyfully—because they follow the cloud more than the crowd.

These are the saints who serve in the shadows.

The hands that lift the church.

The cloud-followers who help God's people move forward.

And then—there's Charon, my wife.

When we first started dating, I asked if she could ever see herself married to a preacher. She answered honestly and directly: "*No.*" Years later, when asked about full-time ministry, she said serving in other ways was enough.

But when the call came—a real call, marked by sacrifice and surrender—she said *yes*. And she's kept saying yes.

Across seven states, Charon has poured herself out for the mission: discipling women, mentoring teens, strengthening marriages, guiding families, and raising up the next generation. Her gifts are clear—vision, leadership, discernment—but she doesn't lead to be seen. She leads to build. And everywhere she's gone, lives have been changed.

The greatest beneficiary of her service?

That would be me—though our three sons might argue otherwise.

These are just a few of the towel-carriers in my life. They remind me that real greatness doesn't wear a title.

It picks up a towel.

And here's the truth:

You know people like this, too.

People whose love shows up in casseroles and phone calls, grocery runs and hospital visits.

People whose names aren't printed—but whose fingerprints are everywhere.

They may never preach a sermon, but they live one daily.

They don't serve to be seen.

They serve because they see.

Following the Cloud Means Following the Towel

To follow the cloud is to follow Christ.

And to follow Christ is to serve.

That's not advanced faith. That's not elite Christianity.

That's real discipleship.

Which means it's the only kind of Christianity that actually counts.
We can't claim to follow Jesus while ignoring the people He died for.
We can't study His words and ignore His ways.
We can't pursue His blessings and bypass His burdens.
We can't claim closeness with God while staying far from the needs He sees.

"Whoever claims to live in him must live as Jesus did." — 1 John 2:6

If we're not following His example — we're not following Him.
And maybe — just maybe — this is what the Church needs most right now.
Not louder arguments.
Not cleverer opinions.
Not another round of theological arm-wrestling over nonessentials.
What if professing believers prioritized serving more than they prioritized winning debates?
What if Christians were known more for carrying towels than carrying grudges?
Imagine that kind of witness.
Not one that shouts — but one that stoops.
Because the cloud is still moving — and it's still bending low.

Others Have Said It, Too

"The best way to find yourself is to lose yourself in the service of others."
— *Mahatma Gandhi*

"Preach the gospel at all times. When necessary, use words."
— *St. Francis of Assisi*

"Life's most persistent and urgent question is, 'What are you doing for others?'"
— *Dr. Martin Luther King Jr.*

Their faith traditions may differ, but they each echo what Jesus made unmistakably clear:

Love looks like service. Greatness looks like humility. And real power is found in pouring yourself out.

Scripture Says It Even Stronger

"Whoever wants to become great among you must be your servant, and whoever wants to be first must be your slave—just as the Son of Man did not come to be served, but to serve, and to give His life as a ransom for many."
— Matthew 20:26–28

"Do nothing out of selfish ambition or vain conceit. Rather, in humility value others above yourselves… In your relationships with one another, have the same mindset as Christ Jesus…"
— Philippians 2:3–5

"If anyone has material possessions and sees a brother or sister in need but has no pity on them, how can the love of God be in that person? Dear children, let us not love with words or speech but with actions and in truth."
— 1 John 3:17–18

Want to know if your life is aligned with the presence of God?
Look at your hands.
Are they clenched?
Or are they carrying a towel?
Because the cloud doesn't just lead you upward.
It leads you downward.
To people. To pain. To places where grace can be felt and love can be known.

The Servant Disciple

Levi didn't start with theology.

He started with a table.

He didn't wait until he was ready.

He opened his home and used what he had.

He said yes — and then he served.

And that yes led him not only to a dinner party… but to a whole new life.

The same man who once collected taxes for Rome would later collect testimonies of Jesus and pen them for the world to see.

The same hands that once reached for coins would later write the very words of the Gospel that now reach the nations.

Because that's what happens when you follow the cloud.

It leads you into rooms you never expected to enter.

It calls you to serve people you once ignored.

And it transforms your yes into a life that multiplies.

Levi didn't just walk behind Jesus.

He watched Him kneel.

He watched Him wash feet.

He watched Him carry a cross.

And over time, he learned to carry the towel too.

This is the journey of every true disciple:

To wrap the towel around your waist.

And to do it not for applause — but for the love of the One who knelt for us first.

So now the question is yours to answer:

Where is the cloud leading you?

Who's sitting at your table?

And are you willing to kneel?

Because **this is real discipleship.**

And real disciples serve.

CLOUD MARKER

If you follow the cloud, you will eventually find a towel in your hands.

Prayer Prompt

Lord,

You did not come to be served, but to serve—and I want to follow where You lead.

Soften my heart and sharpen my sight.

Help me see the needs in front of me—

at home, at work, in my neighborhood, in my church.

Do not let my surrender remain invisible.

Let it take shape in love that kneels, listens, and lifts.

Teach me to carry the towel with joy.

Where You go, I will go.

Where You kneel, I choose to kneel.

In Jesus' name, amen.

Reflection Questions

1. Who are the "least of these" in your daily life—not far away, but close enough to overlook?

2. Has your yes to God expressed itself in visible, sacrificial service—or mostly in intention?

3. What fears, insecurities, or excuses keep you from serving consistently?

4. Who are the towel carriers in your life, and what does their example teach you about true greatness?

5. How has God shaped your story, gifts, and experiences to meet real needs in others?

Live It Out

This week, serve someone **intentionally—and quietly**.

Pick up the towel in a way that brings no recognition, no applause, and no return.

Then ask:

- What did this reveal about my heart?
- What did it show me about Jesus?

Repeat the practice until it becomes instinct.

Because the way of the Cloud is always the way of the Towel.

CHAPTER 15

AS YOU GO

From the Cloud to the Commission

"Therefore, go and make disciples of all nations,"

— MATTHEW 28:19

The same Presence that knelt to serve now rises to send.

From the Towel to the Nations

When you first opened this book, we stood together at the edge of a wilderness dawn — eyes lifted, watching the cloud of God's presence rise and lead His people forward. We learned early on that trust doesn't begin with a map. It begins with Presence. With a God who goes ahead, who guides step by step, who moves and invites His people to move with Him.

And now, here at the end, the movement continues.

In the last chapter, we watched Jesus kneel with a towel and a basin — the same God who led Israel in a pillar of cloud now stooping low to wash feet no one else wanted to touch. We remembered that genuine discipleship doesn't cling to status. It bends. It serves. It reaches into the places where need is real, and dignity feels forgotten.

But the story doesn't stop at the towel.

Because the same Presence that knelt to serve is the Presence that now rises to send.

When God truly leads you, it never stops at stirring your heart — it stretches through your hands. It shapes your worship, yes, but it also widens your world. It moves you toward people. Toward compassion. Toward mission.

And now comes the next step — the movement the whole book has been leading you toward:

The same Jesus who knelt to serve is the One who sends you out.

Not away from service — but deeper into it.

Not away from His presence — but with it.

Carrying His heart into places your feet haven't gone yet.

And for me, that movement began long before I knew what to call it.

Personalizing the Most Famous Verse in the Bible

Growing up in Sunday School every week, I learned to memorize this popular verse:

"For God so loved the world that He gave His one and only Son, that whoever believes in Him shall not perish but have eternal life."

Back then, those words were meaningful — but not as meaningful as they would later become. John 3:16 was familiar. Easy to recite.

But as I grew older… as life happened… as my faith matured… something shifted.

Little by little, the verse I'd memorized became the anchor of truth that began to remake me.

When I realized the cross of Christ wasn't just a symbol of sacrifice but a receipt — proof that my debt was paid in full…

When the blur of childhood religion faded, and Jesus came into sharp, unavoidable focus…

When I stopped talking about God's love for the whole world in general and started personalizing it…

When it sank in that God didn't just love the masses — He loved me...

When it hit: God so *loved* Daryl.

And even more — God so *liked* Daryl.

God wanted me — even after I had grown too familiar with my own faults, flaws, and failures... the very things that fed guilt, shame, and a shrinking sense of worth.

That truth didn't just comfort me.

It cracked something open.

It healed hidden wounds I didn't know I had.

It stirred something in me that had been quiet for too long.

I had to tell somebody — family, friends, classmates, strangers.

I wanted the whole world to know.

When I Realized the Power of this Good News up Close

I'll never forget one of the impactful moments I realized just how powerful the gospel becomes when people encounter it clearly — especially people you know and love.

After college, I started reconnecting with some of my high school friends, inviting them to visit church and, more importantly, to open the Scriptures for themselves. One of my closest friends, Chuck, said yes.

Now, if you knew Chuck back then, you wouldn't have pegged him as someone who'd be interested in God, church, or the Bible. But when he started reading the Gospels — really reading them — something ignited in him. I still remember the moment it broke through. After watching Jesus move through the pages with compassion, authority, and love, Chuck got so excited he blurted out, without thinking, "Daryl... this is some good s*#t!"

He didn't even realize he'd said it. I just laughed, nodded, and told him he was absolutely right — God *is* incredible.

Not long after that, Chuck gave his life to Christ and was baptized. A few weeks later, his wife, Paula, made the same decision. That was over thirty-eight years ago. And to this day, their love for God, their passion for sharing Christ, and their service to others are unmatched. You'd be hard-pressed to find a couple more evangelistic and devoted to Jesus. Heaven only knows the depth of their impact on people's lives.

That moment marked me. It taught me something simple and profound:

When people meet Jesus directly in the Gospels, their lives change.

You don't need a polished presentation.

You don't need a seminary education.

You don't need all the answers.

Just open the Scriptures (especially the gospels).

Share the good news.

And let God do what only He can do.

In Jesus, and through the cross, sins are forgiven.

In trusting Him as Lord, eternal life begins.

And many of my friends responded by giving their lives to Christ.

That's what happens when the gospel becomes real.

You don't just believe it — you move because of it.

You don't just receive it — you respond.

And the same cloud of grace that covered you… is rising again.

Not just to lead you out — but to send you forward.

God Is Still on the Move

What kind of God moves like this — not just in glory, but in grace?

We saw it back in Exodus, when God revealed His heart in the cleft of the rock:

"The Lord, the Lord, the compassionate and gracious God, slow to anger, abounding in love and faithfulness, maintaining love to thousands, and forgiving wickedness, rebellion and sin." — Exodus 34:6–7

Remember — that's what filled the cloud.

Not just fire and smoke — but mercy.

Presence. A heart that longed to walk with His people and bring them all the way home.

Centuries later, that same God came closer. Compassion took on flesh.

"Jesus went through all the towns and villages, teaching in their syna-gogues, proclaiming the good news of the kingdom and healing every disease and sickness. When he saw the crowds, he had compassion on them, because they were harassed and helpless, like sheep without a shepherd." — Matthew 9:35–36

That was the cloud moving again —
not over the tabernacle, but through the streets.
Not above the people, but among them.
Same heart.
Same mission.
Same movement.
That's what we've traced throughout this book — from Sinai to Galilee, from the pillar of cloud to the person of Christ. The God who led with presence has always led with compassion.
Still moved by suffering.
Still stirred by lostness.
Still full of mercy, truth, and purpose.
And now… He's still moving.

When You Say "Yes, Completely Yes," Jesus Commissions You

When you say yes to Jesus, you're not just stepping into grace — you're stepping into purpose.
You're not just saved from something — you're called to something.
Jesus never separates salvation from commission.
His call is always both invitation and mission.
Grace doesn't just catch you — it sends you.
This is what He said from the very beginning:

"Come, follow Me, and I will make you become fishers of men."
— Mark 1:17 (NASB)

The first recorded words Jesus spoke to His disciples were a call to transformation and vocation:

Follow Me… and I will make you.

Follow Me… and I'll give you a new identity.

Follow Me… and I'll shape you into something you could never become without Me.

Follow Me… and I'll use your life to change lives.

You don't need to wait for a title, a platform, or a position to be used by God.

Your calling didn't start when you got it all together — it started the moment you said yes.

And just like the cloud didn't stop moving when Israel entered the wilderness, the Spirit doesn't stop moving once you've begun to follow.

He is still leading.

Still shaping.

Still sending.

When you said yes to Jesus, He said yes to using you.

The fisherman became a disciple.

The tax collector became an apostle.

The skeptic became a witness.

The sinner became a messenger.

And you?

You became a sent one.

You were never meant to just be rescued.

You were meant to be released.

Jesus gives you a purpose that outlasts your paycheck… outshines your résumé… and leaves an imprint time cannot erase — a purpose that echoes in heaven.

That's what people are aching for, whether they realize it or not —

Not just pleasure.

Not just success.

But significance. Eternal significance.

A reason to wake up that's bigger than your name and deeper than your timeline.

And Jesus says, "I have that for you. Come. Follow Me."

The same Presence that called you out is the One who now says:

"Let's go testify about the good news and teach people to be My disciples."

Matthew Got It — And He Wrote It Down

The one who once sat behind a tax booth…

The one Jesus called with a simple "Follow me" …

The one who left everything behind to step into the yes…

He was there on the mountain.

And now, years later, he's the one writing it down:

"Then Jesus came to them and said, 'All authority in heaven and on earth has been given to Me.'" — Matthew 28:18

When Matthew wrote the Great Commission, he wasn't just reporting about history — he was remembering his personal encounter with Christ.

The Rabbi who had first called him out of the crowd was now commissioning him into the world.

He had experienced the grace.

He had followed the cloud.

And now he was being sent with the message—to call others to do the same.

This wasn't theory.

It was testimony.

The man who once felt most disqualified was now helping others find their yes in Christ.

And he knew — this message wasn't just for the eleven.

It was for all of us.

This Is the Mission — Make Disciples

They had seen the nails.

Heard the cry.

Watched the tomb sealed.

And now — Jesus was standing before them.

Alive. Radiant. Risen.

The cross looked like the end.

But this?

This was the beginning.

The risen King wasn't just proving His victory — He was announcing their mission.

"All authority ... has been given to Me." — Matthew 28:18

Before Jesus sent them, He grounded them.

All authority.

Every realm.

Every people.

Every generation.

No sphere lies outside His rule.

No heart lies beyond His reach.

And from that place of absolute authority, He gave the command that would echo across the ages:

"Therefore, go and make disciples of all nations..." — Matthew 28:19

The Greek word is *mathēteusate* — a verb, not a title.

Not "collect converts."

Not "gather admirers."

Not "get people to agree with your doctrine."

Disciple.

Mathēteusate means to train, form, and shape someone into a follower who becomes like the Master.

In the first century, a *mathētēs* wasn't a casual learner — but an apprentice who patterned their entire way of life after their teacher.

So when Jesus said, "Disciple all nations," He wasn't talking about borders.

The word *ethnē* means peoples — every ethnicity, every culture, every group, every kind of person.

Jesus was calling His followers to invite people into a transforming relationship with Him:

Walk with Him.

Learn His ways.

Imitate His life.

Be changed by His presence.

And this mission wasn't given to clergy or professionals.

It was given to every believer.

"As you go…"

In Greek, it means: **as you live.**

Wherever your feet take you, the mission goes too.

Your neighborhood.

Your job.

Your campus.

Your everyday conversations.

This is — and always has been — the calling of every follower of Jesus.

A New Identity: Out with the Old, In with the New

"…baptizing them in the name of the Father and of the Son and of the Holy Spirit…" — Matthew 28:19b

When someone believes —

When someone says yes —

Jesus doesn't leave the first step up for debate.

Baptize them.

Not as ritual.

Not as optional symbol.

But as surrender.

As beginning.

Paul put it this way:

"We were therefore buried with Him through baptism into death in order that, just as Christ was raised from the dead through the glory of the Father, we too may live a new life." — Romans 6:4

Baptism is burial.
And resurrection.
Burial of pride, sin, and old ways.
Resurrection into grace, identity, and purpose.
Paul said it another way:

"Therefore, if anyone is in Christ, the new creation has come: The old has gone, the new is here!" — 2 Corinthians 5:17

To be baptized "in the name" means total identification with the Father, Son, and Spirit.
Matthew knew what that meant.
He had once been marked by Rome.
Branded by betrayal.
Defined by a booth.
But now — he was marked by heaven.
No longer "Matthew the tax collector."
Now: "Matthew, follower of Jesus."
Disciple. Witness. Gospel writer.
And he knew baptism wasn't the finish line.
It was the starting line.

This Is a Whole-Life Transformation

"Teaching them to obey everything I have commanded you." — Matthew 28:20a

Not fans.
Followers.
Not observers.

Obeyers.

Jesus summed His commands simply:

Love God with everything.

Love your neighbor as yourself.

Discipleship isn't quick or transactional.

It's formation.

It's walking with people.

Feeding, nurturing, guiding them toward maturity — until they can do the same.

Matthew didn't just record Jesus' words — he obeyed them.

And now he calls us to do the same.

This Is a Presence-Powered Mission

"And surely I am with you always, to the very end of the age."
— Matthew 28:20b

Jesus didn't just give them a command.

He gave them a companion.

This mission isn't powered by effort.

It's sustained by Presence.

"I will ask the Father, and He will give you another advocate to help you and be with you forever — the Spirit of truth." — John 14:16–17

The Advocate.

The Comforter.

The Counselor.

The Spirit — not beside us, but within us.

The same voice that called Matthew out of the booth…

now sent him to call others.

The same cloud that led Israel…

now moved through Spirit-filled disciples.

And the same Jesus who rewrote Matthew's story…

now commissioned him to rewrite others.
Because the cloud never stops at comfort.
It moves toward mission.
And now — so do we.

And That Mission Still Stands

The command hasn't changed.
The commission hasn't expired.
And the Presence hasn't faded.
Jesus is still calling.
Still sending.
Still moving.
If you've followed the cloud this far —
If you've said yes to grace, trust, surrender, and formation —
then this is your moment.
Go.
Not in your name — but in His.
Not by your strength — but in His Spirit.
Not for your glory — but for His Kingdom.
Because this isn't just Matthew's mission.
It's yours.

Now It's Your Turn

The cloud doesn't just lead you out.
It sends you forward.
You weren't saved to sit.
You were called to move.
To help others follow the cloud too.
You're part of the movement that started on a Galilean mountain —
when Jesus looked His disciples in the eyes and said:
"Go make disciples."
This is how the cloud moves now:
Through people.
Through you.

I'll never forget when grace broke through my head and hit my heart, and I couldn't stay in the booth of comfort anymore. I had to go — to teammates, dorm mates, family, new friends, old friends, anyone God put in my path.

That's what the Great Commission does:

It turns ordinary people into messengers.

The Cloud Is Still on the Move

The story didn't end with Matthew.

And it doesn't end with you.

Because the cloud hasn't stopped moving.

The same Presence that led Israel…

The same mercy that walked Galilee's streets…

The same Spirit that filled disciples with fire…

is still leading today.

And He's leading you.

Not with a map, but with Himself.

Not toward comfort but calling.

Not just for your growth, but for His glory.

So don't drift.

Don't go back.

Don't settle.

Follow the cloud — even when the way is unfamiliar.

Even when the crowd roars.

Even when clarity disappears.

Because the cloud still moves —

and now it moves through you.

So, go.

Help someone else find their way.

Follow the cloud.

Help others follow it too.

Trust God's lead —

and don't let the world pull you away.

The God who brought you this far

will go with you, as you go.

Lift Your Eyes — The Cloud Rises Again

Picture it.

A wilderness dawn.

The camp still.

The horizon pale with new light.

Then you look up.

There it is —

the cloud that sheltered you, steadied you, protected you —

now beginning to rise.

A stirring.

A rising.

A glow like Sinai waking up again.

The camp shifts.

People rise.

Hearts quicken.

This is the moment.

You gather your things — not because you've mastered the map,

but because you trust the Guide who holds it.

You take your first step — not because the road is clear,

but because the Presence is near.

And the truth hits you:

This is the same Presence that led Moses…

that called Peter onto the waves…

that found Matthew in a booth…

that carried you through desert, fog, fire, silence, and surrender.

And now — that Presence is moving through you.

Calling you.

Sending you.

Commissioning you.

So lift your eyes.

The cloud is rising again.

Go where it goes.

Speak where it leads.

Love who it loves.

Disciple who it sends you to.
Carry the towel.
Carry the cross.
Carry the message.
Because the story isn't finished —
and He has written you into the next chapter.
Lift your eyes.
The cloud is on the move.
And now… so are you.

CLOUD MARKER

**The same cloud that brought you out
is the cloud that sends you on.**

Prayer Prompt

Lord,
   You led me with mercy.
   You guarded me in the fog.
   You caught me with grace.
   You called me to follow.
   Now send me.
   I don't want to just believe—I want to obey.
   I don't want to only receive—I want to go and give.
   Give me courage to trust Your voice over the crowd's,
   to keep walking even when the path feels unclear,
   and to help others follow You as I follow You.
   Here I am.
   Use me.
   Amen.

Reflection Questions

1. What specific "yes" has God been placing before you—personally, spiritually, or missionally?
2. Where do you sense the cloud moving right now—and how are you responding to it?
3. Who in your life needs help learning to follow Jesus, not just hearing about Him?
4. What fears, comforts, or distractions threaten to keep you from full obedience to the Great Commission?
5. What would it look like for you to *go intentionally* as a disciple-maker in your current season?

Live It Out

Commissioned.

Set aside five minutes this week and write out your personal *yes* to Jesus. Include:

- what you are leaving behind,
- what you are stepping into,
- and who you sense God calling you to reach.

Pray over it.
Seal it.
Then live it.
The cloud is moving.
And you are sent.

Give It Away — One Last Word

If this book has helped you follow the cloud, don't let it stop with you.

Pass it on to someone who feels stuck, someone searching, someone who needs to know that God still guides — and still goes with them.

Let it be more than a book.

Let it be a seed of hope.

A breadcrumb trail to the Presence.

A conversation starter for trust to take root.

Because what God has done in you, He intends to do through you.

That's how the cloud moves now — not just above His people, but through them.

So when you turn the last page, take the next step:

Give it away.

Start a conversation.

Invite someone to follow the cloud with you.

And trust that the same God who has led you this far

will use your yes to lead someone else home.

Because the story isn't over —

and now, it moves through you.

CONTINUE THE JOURNEY

DON'T LET THE journey stop at the final page.

The cloud still rises.

The same Presence who led Israel, who walked among us in flesh, who calls you to surrender and sends you into service — He is still moving. Trust is formed step by step.

If you want to keep growing:

- Receive **Still Waters: A 7-Day Quiet Time Journey through Psalm 23**
- Access additional Scripture-rooted reflections
- Stay connected to future resources and teaching
- Explore ways to bring this message to your church or community

Find everything at:
darylreed.com

If these pages strengthened your trust, I would be honored to stay connected.

Keep your eyes on the cloud.

BRING THE CLOUD TO YOUR COMMUNITY

THIS MESSAGE WAS never meant to sit on a shelf.

It was meant to move through a people.

If *Follow the Cloud, Not the Crowd* strengthened your trust, bring it into your church, leadership team, or small group.

Use it as:

- A 6–8 week study
- A sermon series
- A leadership resource
- A discipleship pathway
- A retreat framework

Each chapter includes a Cloud Marker, reflection questions, prayer prompts, and a clear Live It Out step — ready to lead.

A simple rhythm:

1. Pray
2. Read the Cloud Marker
3. Discuss
4. Choose one Live It Out step
5. Pray again

Churches and ministries may request bulk copies at:
darylreed.com

The cloud never gathered spectators.
It formed a people.
Don't just follow it.
Lead others to follow it too.

ACKNOWLEDGMENTS

TO THE GOD who still leads with a cloud — thank You for meeting me in every season and shaping these words long before I wrote them.

To my wife, Charon — God's gift to me. You make me better. Thank you for your steady encouragement, your patience through long writing days, and your unwavering belief in this message. You have been strength beside me in every step.

To my mother, Sharon Reed — thank you for introducing me to God, the church, and the Scriptures. Your faith still steadies me.

To my father — thank you for the foundation you laid and the example you set. I wish you were here to see the fruit of your work in me.

To my sons, Cameron, Harrison, and Wynston — the depth of my love for you is only a shadow of His. Being your pops is one of the greatest joys of my life.

To my siblings, Larry and Terri — and to Damian, whom I miss more than words can hold — thank you for the gift of growing up together.

To my grandparents — I am a product of your courage and faithfulness.

To our extended family — your love has been a steady gift.

To my circle — Carlos and Cassandra, Abou and Contina, Ray and Tawana, Darryl and Lupi, Wayne and Tammy — thank you for allowing God to use you in my life.

To DC Regional Christian Church — my spiritual family. Thank you for trusting me, refining me, and walking with me as we seek to follow the presence of God together.

To the friends, mentors, and leaders who encouraged this work — thank you for your prayers, conversations, and conviction that this message needed to be written.

To Kevin and Trae — thank you for believing in Charon and me and entrusting us with ministry through the years.

To Ron and Lavonia — thank you for loving our young family and helping shape us for ministry.

To all who have prayed, spoken a timely word, or walked alongside me — your fingerprints are woven through these pages.

Thank you.

ABOUT THE AUTHOR

DARYL REED has served in ministry for more than 35 years, learning—often the hard way—to trust God through both clarity and fog. He currently serves as Lead Minister of DC Regional Christian Church, helping people recognize and respond to God's leading in the real, everyday moments of life.

Follow the Cloud, Not the Crowd is rooted in Scripture and shaped by a lifetime of discovering one essential truth: God always goes first—and we are invited to move with Him. Through seasons of leadership, failure, growth, and grace, Daryl has learned that God's presence is not simply comfort; it is the power that carries us forward.

He lives in the Washington, D.C. area with his wife, Charon, who has faithfully walked beside him for decades as they have poured their lives into helping people follow Jesus. Together, they invest in young adults, encourage leaders, mentor couples, and watch God change lives—often one conversation at a time. He is the grateful father of three sons who continue to teach him as much about faith as he has ever taught.

In quieter moments, he returns to this conviction: the cloud is still moving—and God is still leading.